DATE DUE

PROJECTS FOR YOUNG SCIENTISTS

ASTRONOMY AND PLANETOLOGY

BY NECIA H. APFEL

FRANKLIN WATTS

NEW YORK I LONDON I TORONTO I SYDNEY I 1983

Diagrams by Vantage Art, Inc.

Photographs courtesy of the Adler Planetarium,
Chicago: pp. 8, 11, and 29; Yerkes Observatory:
p. 17; Palomar Observatory: pp. 18, 23, 25, 30,
and 103; National Radio Astronomy Observatory,
operated by Associated Universities, Inc., under
contract with the National Science Foundation:
p. 22; Mount Wilson Observatory: pp. 39, 99, and
110; NASA: pp. 45, 49, 50 (with the Jet Propulsion
Laboratory at the California Institute of Technology),
54 (with the Jet Propulsion Laboratory at the
California Institute of Technology), 56, 58, 61,
and 66; n.c.: pp. 77, 106; Lick Observatory: p. 109.

Library of Congress Cataloging in Publication Data

Apfel, Necia H.
Astronomy and planetology.

Includes index.
Summary: Gives instructions for building or making
theodolites, sundials, telescopes, spectroscopes, planetariums,
and models of stars, and describes methods and times for
observing the sun, moon, planets, stars, comets, and meteors.
1. Astronomy—Experiments—Juvenile literature.
2. Astronomical instruments—Juvenile literature.
3. Planetology—Juvenile literature.   [1. Astronomy—
Experiments.   2. Astronomical instruments.
3. Planetology.   4. Space sciences.   5. Experiments]
I. Title. II. Title: Projects for young scientists.
QB46.A63 1983   522   83-3476
ISBN 0-531-04668-0

CONTENTS

INTRODUCTION 1

Chapter One
BUILDING A THEODOLITE 5

Chapter Two
SUNDIALS 10
The Analemma 15

Chapter Three
TELESCOPE-MAKING 16
The Optical Telescope 16
Radio Telescopes 21

Chapter Four
THE CONSTRUCTION
AND USE OF
A SPECTROSCOPE 24

Chapter Five
BUILDING A PLANETARIUM 28

Chapter Six

MODEL CONSTRUCTION 32

The Milky Way 32
Our Place in Space 33
Stellar Structure: A Model Star 34

Chapter Seven

OBSERVING THE SUN 37

Photographing the Sun 41
Spectroscopic Observation of the Sun 41
The Sun's Radiation 42

Chapter Eight

OBSERVING THE MOON 44

The Lunar Eclipse 46
The Moon Illusion 47
The Lunar Surface 47
Cratering 48

Chapter Nine

OBSERVING THE PLANETS 52

The Martian "Riverbeds" 59
Those Mysterious Canals of Mars 62
The Moons of Jupiter 63

Chapter Ten

MEASURING THE EARTH'S CIRCUMFERENCE 67

Why Aren't Planets Spherical? 71

Chapter Eleven

COMETS AND METEORS 73

Meteor Showers 79

Chapter Twelve

TINY PARTICLES 83

Collecting Micrometeorites 83
Detection of Cosmic Rays 86

Chapter Thirteen

VARIABLE STARS 89

Chapter Fourteen

THE TIMING OF OCCULTATIONS 94

Chapter Fifteen

"STAR GAUGING" THE MILKY WAY 98

Chapter Sixteen

BLINKING 101

Chapter Seventeen

ADDITIONAL IDEAS 105

Astrophotography 105
Archeoastronomy 107
Potpourri 107

Chapter Eighteen

CONTESTS AND COMPETITIONS 112

The Priscilla and Bart Bok Awards 113
The Westinghouse Science Talent Search 114
The Space Shuttle and You 115

APPENDIX 116

INDEX 120

INTRODUCTION

Each year, all across the United States, thousands of schools have science fairs. For months, students work on experiments, build exhibits, and read research material in preparation for the fair. Each chooses some scientific or engineering subject to study in depth.

When your school has such a fair, you, too, may be called upon to present a project. And your first major question will be: What do I study?

Space science is not chosen by the majority of students, probably because they don't realize how many projects can be done in this field. And some of these projects can actually help professional astronomers by providing much-needed data. This is rarely true in any other field.

Most people believe that research in astronomy, and in the relatively new, more narrow field of planetology (the study of the planets in our solar system), requires large telescopes and sophisticated equipment. But there are a great many projects possible with small telescopes or even binoculars, and many more that can be done with a camera or even the naked eye.

In this book you will find suggestions for such projects. Some are very simple; others are more complicated. Some need very little equipment, whereas others will require access to a laboratory or an observatory or possibly expensive instruments. These factors should certainly enter into your choice of a topic.

You will also find that some of the experiments are described in great detail, whereas others are just outlines or suggested lines of research. Remember that one of the criteria of a good project is its originality. Therefore, even if you follow one of the detailed experiments, you must add something of your own, whether it be procedure, instrumentation, or special analysis, in order to make it a worthwhile project.

Most important in deciding what project to do is your own interest in the subject. Is there an area that you would like to learn more about? Did some aspect of an astronomy unit in your science class spark your curiosity? Perhaps you saw an eclipse or viewed a space launch or visited a planetarium and want to find out more about what you experienced.

You must remember, however, that astronomy is a unique science. In most of the other scientific fields, experiments can be designed and carried out in a laboratory. Such experiments can be repeated over and over again by many different observers. In astronomy, the "experiments" are not usually set up by a scientist in a laboratory. You cannot change the stars or planets. You usually can't have a "control" group.

The experiments are events that occur millions or billions of miles away. The astronomer's job is to devise ways to observe these events and then to explain them. Careful observations and measurements are of major importance in this field. Accurate instruments capable of such tasks are essential.

Once the data has been gathered, the scientist must organize it and then communicate the results of the study to the rest of the scientific community. Preparing a written report is part of this communication process. It must answer such questions as: What do other scientists want to know about this study? What is being demonstrated or proven? What are the limitations of the study regarding its accuracy? What is the error range in the measurements that have been made?

It is very important that a scientist be faithful in reporting exactly what is observed. No attempt should be made to conform to any supposed "right answer." A discussion of possible sources and ranges of error is invaluable.

In doing your experiment, keep all your original records and measurements. You might consider using a diary to enter all your procedures, ideas, and materials used. Number and date all observations and photographs and also note their existence in your diary. All of this record-keeping will help you when you are ready to write your final report. Unless you have only a small amount of data, you will want to reduce your data to graphs and charts. Otherwise, your final report will get too bulky and cumbersome.

All scientific reports or projects should include:

1. The project objective: What are you trying to demonstrate or prove?
2. Instruments and equipment used; materials used; sources of information consulted.
3. Method of observation or demonstration.
4. Recorded observations; these should include maps, charts, graphs, photographs, and diagrams. Each observation must have the data and time and a comment about the conditions of observation.
5. Discussion of the error range in the measurements.
6. Analysis or conclusion: What information was derived? How was this conclusion reached? How accurate is it?

There are three types of projects that can be done in the field of astronomy:

1. *Observation.* This usually requires a telescope or a good pair of binoculars and an area of the country in which a large portion of the sky is unobstructed. A camera on a sturdy tripod or attached to the telescope is essential in some projects.
2. *Construction.* The instrument to be used is first constructed as part of the project and then tested for accuracy and for informational value.
3. *Demonstration.* A theory or concept is explained with the use of models, diagrams, computer programs, etc.

Now let's look at some space science projects.

1

BUILDING A
THEODOLITE

The theodolite was an instrument used by medieval astronomers to measure how many degrees a given celestial body was above the horizon. Many theodolites were ornately decorated and made of precious metals. Today, the sextant has replaced the theodolite as a measuring instrument.

However, both the sextant and the theodolite measure only the altitude of an object. A simple instrument similar to a surveyor's theodolite can be built that will measure not only the altitude but also the azimuth of the object. To make it you will need:

a half-circle protractor at least 6 inches (15 cm) in diameter

a full-circle protractor at least 6 inches (15 cm) in diameter

a plastic straw or small tube (a peashooter, perhaps?)

a small piece of cardboard or thin plywood

a plumb line (a piece of thread attached to a metal washer is adequate)

a square piece of wood ½ to 1 inch (1.25 to 2.5 cm) thick for the base (It must be larger in area than the full-circle protractor.)

an 8- to 12-inch-long (20- to 30-cm) piece of wood for the upright (It should be at least 1″ × 1″ (2.5 × 2.5 cm) thick to support the rest of the instrument.)
metal screws

Cut the cardboard or thin plywood into the shape of a pointer. Paint or color it a bright color. Glue it to the bottom of the upright so that its pointed end sticks out.

Position the full-circle protractor in the center of the base and glue it in place. With a screw, attach the upright to the center of the full-circle protractor so that the upright can be turned around.

Glue the straw or tube to the flat edge of the half-circle protractor. You may have to first attach the protractor to a thin piece of wood to give the straw more space upon which to lie.

Fasten the center of the protractor to the upright with a screw so that it is movable. Tie the plumb line to this screw, making sure that the washer or other weight hangs down freely in front of the protractor.

Place the theodolite on a table or other level surface. Orient it so that the 0° mark on the base protractor is in line with true north. You can do this by sighting the North Star (Polaris) through the tube. It is important not to move the base from this position during your other sightings of stars or other celestial bodies.

Swing the upright around clockwise and adjust the straw up or down to sight a given star. The star's altitude is determined by reading the number of degrees directly behind the thread on the half-circle protractor. Azimuth is the number of degrees that the pointer indicates on the full-circle protractor. That is how far you had to turn the upright away from the 0° mark to sight the star.

Use a small flashlight covered with red tissue paper or cellophane to help keep your night vision while you take your readings. If you want to take readings on the sun,

A Model Theodolite

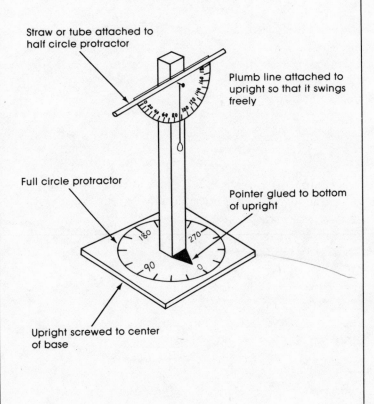

Straw or tube attached to half circle protractor

Plumb line attached to upright so that it swings freely

Full circle protractor

Pointer glued to bottom of upright

Upright screwed to center of base

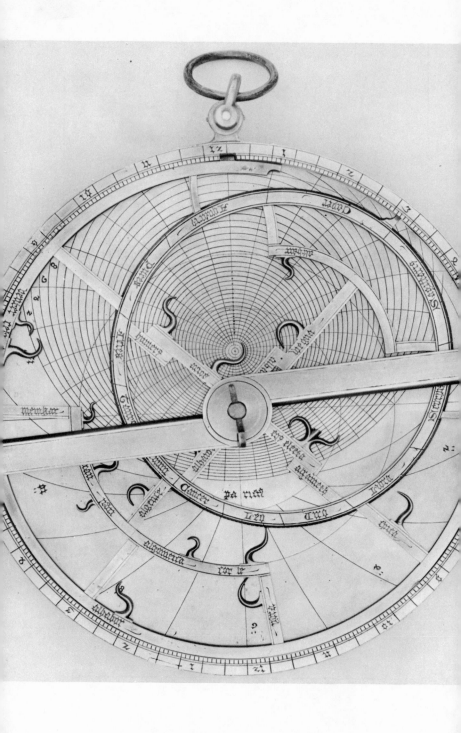

angle the straw until the sunlight shines down it onto a white piece of paper, making a small, sharp circle. DO NOT LOOK DIRECTLY AT THE SUN.

This working model of a theodolite can be used in several science projects. However, if your project consists solely of constructing and using it, you should make it out of much more durable materials. For example, a thin metal tubing should replace the straw, and all wooden parts should be smoothly finished. There are other ancient instruments that also can be constructed and demonstrated as part of the same project. These might include an armillary sphere, an orrery, an astrolabe, or a sundial.

You may also be able to add to the theodolite so that you can find a star's right ascension (R.A.) or declination (Decl.), or knowing these coordinates, locate a celestial body. This is especially valuable in finding stars too faint to be seen without a telescope.

THIS BRONZE ASTROLABE WAS MADE IN PARIS AROUND 1395 BY JEAN FUSORIS.

2

SUNDIALS

There are many different types of sundials that can be constructed. You will find designs for sundials in books for amateur astronomers. There are also entire books on building sundials. Here is a very simple design that requires very little equipment.

First, you must determine your latitude on the earth. One way of doing this is to measure the altitude of the North Star (Polaris). The altitude of the North Star is equal to your latitude. Thus, if the North Star is 40° above the horizon, you are at 40° north latitude.

From a piece of thin plywood, cut out a right triangle with one angle equal to your latitude. The third angle will, of course, be 90° minus your latitude. This triangular piece is the "gnomon" of the sundial. Attach the gnomon upright to a flat board so that the "latitude angle" and the right angle are lying on the board.

Place the sundial in a sunny spot, with the hypotenuse of the gnomon pointing toward the North Star. To do this during the day, you must first determine your north-south direction. You can use a compass, although the compass needle actually points to the North Magnetic Pole and not to the North Pole. This difference is very small unless you are very far north. At night you can determine how great a discrepancy there is by comparing the compass nee-

BRASS AND MARBLE SUNDIAL MADE
IN VIENNA, AUSTRIA, IN 1742

A simple sundial

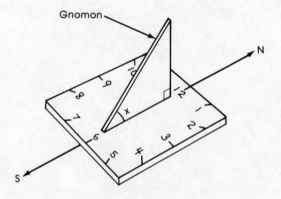

Angle X equals your latitude.

dle's direction with the direction of the North Star (Polaris).

As the shadow of the gnomon falls on different parts of the baseboard, mark off the hours and half-hours. At noon, the shadow should line up with the northerly direction of the gnomon. However, note that noon on your sundial will not always agree with 12:00 noon on your watch.

Your sundial shows "apparent solar time." This varies slightly throughout the year because the exact length of an apparent solar day varies. We therefore use the "mean solar time," which is based upon the length of the "mean solar day." This is the average length of an apparent solar day. The difference between apparent and mean solar time is called the "equation of time." This difference can be almost as great as 16½ minutes.

If you know how much the equation of time is for a particular day, you can use your sundial and the following formula to determine mean solar time: apparent time minus mean time equals equation of time. Or, using your sundial and a watch, you can make a chart of the equation of time throughout the year.

Remember, however, that your clock time is the standard for your entire time zone. Your location within this zone will also affect the difference between sundial and clock time, but at least this amount doesn't vary. For example, if the equation of time for a particular day is 4^m (four minutes), the sun will be on the meridian at Greenwich, England, at 12:04. But Chicago, Illinois, unlike Greenwich, is not in the center of its time zone, and therefore a correction of -10^m must be used to determine when the sun will be on the Chicago meridian. That is when a Chicago-oriented sundial will read 12:00. Data for the equation of time and for longitude corrections can be found in the *Observer's Handbook*. Remember also to take Daylight Saving Time into account if you are observing during the summertime.

The Analemma

The Analemma, which is found on many
world globes, indicates for any date
the latitude at which the sun appears
directly overhead at noon as well as
the equation of time for that date.

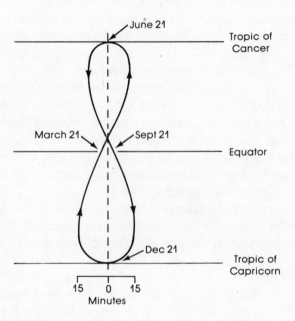

Apparent sun
ahead of mean sun

Apparent sun
behind mean sun

THE ANALEMMA

Using your sundial, note when local noontime occurs. Record the altitude and azimuth of the sun at that time for each date of observation. For this you will need a home-made theodolite (see Chapter One) or some other instrument.

Take a photograph of the sun in the sky at noon on each date of observation. This will require special film and very short exposure times. Be sure to include objects (trees, buildings) in the pictures so that the sun's changing position relative to them can be compared.

If your camera allows you to take double exposures, you may be able to set it up so that you can make an exposure on the same frame every week or so. But then the exposure must be even shorter than before and the aperture of the camera very small. Otherwise, the extreme brilliance of the sun will quickly wash out the picture.

Compare your data and photographs with an anal-emma (these are found on most globes of the earth). If you can follow the noontime sun throughout the entire year, you will see that it does indeed make a "figure eight" in the sky. A full explanation of this phenomenon should be part of your report.

3

TELESCOPE-MAKING

THE OPTICAL TELESCOPE

The construction of an optical telescope is not only an excellent project for a science fair; it may also be the start of a hobby that will give you great pleasure and satisfaction for years to come. Even a beginner can make a telescope that is far superior to those of Galileo's. And one of the top forty finalists in the 15th Science Talent Search conducted by Westinghouse Electric Corporation constructed an 8-inch (20-cm) Cassegrain telescope as her winning project.

With that encouragement, it is still best not to make too large or complex an instrument at first. Start with a 6-inch (15-cm) reflector for best results. Smaller ones don't perform very well unless they are very well made, and larger ones increase the difficulty you will have in handling the finished product. There are several excellent books available on telescope-making, and many planetariums have telescope-making workshops and classes.

The simplest reflecting telescope consists of four major parts:

1. the objective mirror, which collects the light and reflects it to a focus;
2. a flat diagonal mirror, which bends the focused rays at a right angle so that the image can be observed without obstructing the incoming light;

GALILEO'S TELESCOPES, SHOWN HERE,
NOW RESIDE IN THE MUSEUM OF THE
HISTORY OF SCIENCE IN FLORENCE, ITALY.

3. a magnifying lens or eyepiece, through which the image is examined; and
4. a movable framework or mounting, which supports the optical parts and keeps them all in alignment.

The mounting can be any combination of materials that are handy—wood, pipe, sheet metal, or discarded machine parts. Or it can be purchased from a scientific supply house (see the Appendix). Its dimensions will vary according to the size telescope you plan to construct.

Materials for the objective and diagonal mirrors are also available in kit form from the scientific supply houses. These places can also provide the necessary eyepieces, which are relatively inexpensive. Or you can make them if you have the necessary machine tools.

The most important part of the telescope is the objective mirror. Half the cost in time, money, and labor will be used here. The telescope kits include directions on how to grind the objective mirror to the exact shape necessary for your telescope, but if you have never done this before, you will probably require some guidance and assistance. A nearby planetarium or local astronomy club can be of great help here.

Grinding is also a messy job and should be done in a place that is free of dust and has a source of water. If you don't have a nearby planetarium workshop, your basement or garage will probably suffice.

Once the telescope is constructed, you must test its capabilities and accuracy. Most books on telescope-making give instructions on how this can be done. Your project should include your construction procedure and test results.

THE 200-INCH (5-M) HALE TELESCOPE

Optical Telescopes

Refracting Telescope

In *refracting* telescopes, light is gathered by the objective lens, which bends the rays and carries them to the eyepiece, where they are focused by magnifying lenses.

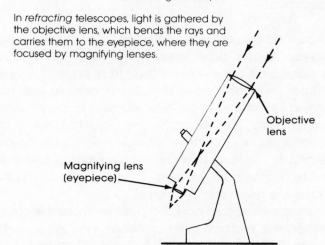

Objective lens

Magnifying lens (eyepiece)

Reflecting Telescope

In *reflecting* telescopes, light comes down the tube and is reflected back by a mirror to a focal point near the top of the tube, where another mirror deflects the light into a hole on the side of the tube.

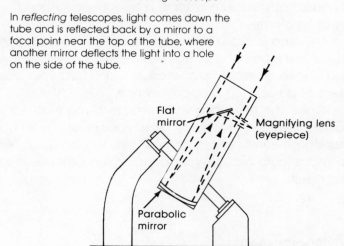

Flat mirror

Magnifying lens (eyepiece)

Parabolic mirror

RADIO TELESCOPES

An entirely new look at the universe was made possible by the development of radio astronomy. Although it is a relatively new field (a little over fifty years old), radio astronomy has in some respects surpassed optical astronomy in surveying the universe.

To build a simple radio telescope, obtain a shortwave radio receiver and fit it with a directional antenna. Then connect the output of the receiver to a voltmeter so that you can measure the intensity of the radiation.

As you move the antenna across the night sky (sweeping the sky), carefully plot the voltmeter readings on a chart. Use the approximate right ascension and declination coordinates for each area recorded.

Use only one frequency with each sweep of the sky. Then repeat the sweep at another frequency, and compare the two charts. Compare your charts with an optical sky chart, and see if you can associate any radio sources with objects or constellations.

During the daytime, determine the radio emissions of the sun at various frequencies. Repeat this method of recording for several weeks to note any fluctuations. Can you find any correlation between the radio emissions and sunspot activity?

In the December 1977 issue of *Astronomy,* a former Westinghouse Science Talent Search winner described the rig that she built as a science-fair project. She also suggested the best frequency ranges on which to concentrate sky sweeps. Several basic reference books on radio astronomy are available as well.

In the March 1982 issue of *Sky and Telescope,* you will find radio maps of the broad structure of the sky. And in the *Observer's Handbook* there is a list of radio sources that can be detected with amateur radio telescopes. Finally, in the March 1983 issue of *Astronomy,* there is an excellent article on how to construct a more sophisticated radio telescope.

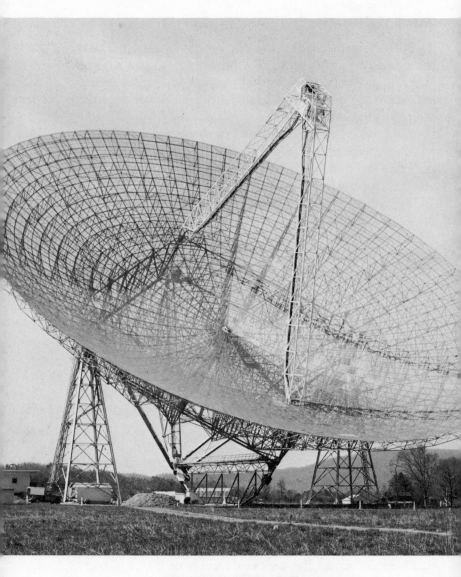

THE 300-FOOT (90-M) TRANSIT
RADIO TELESCOPE AT GREEN BANK,
WEST VIRGINIA. THIS INSTRUMENT
WEIGHS 500 TONS, AND MOST
OF IT IS MOVABLE.

A PECULIAR GALAXY IN CENTAURUS (NGC 5128).
IT IS BELIEVED THAT THIS GALAXY IS ACTUALLY
BEING TORN APART BY SOME VIOLENT EXPLOSION,
WHICH HAS CAUSED IT TO BECOME ONE OF THE MOST
POWERFUL RADIO SOURCES IN THE SOUTHERN SKY.

4

THE CONSTRUCTION AND USE OF A SPECTROSCOPE

The spectroscope is one of the most valuable tools in astronomy. It "breaks up," or diffracts, light into its component colors, or spectrum. This is done with the use of a prism or a very fine grating.

The grating is a thin, flat sheet of material containing thousands of parallel microscopic grooves. In professional observatories, the spectroscope is attached to a telescope with a camera rather than an eyepiece in order to record the stellar spectra. A photograph of the stellar spectrum is called a "spectrogram." The instrument is then called a "spectrograph."

Different types of stars have different spectra. The main reason for these differences is the surface temperatures of the stars. Each star is classified according to its stellar spectrum. Precise stellar classification requires careful analysis of small differences in stellar spectra. If you have access to a manufactured spectrograph or a collection of spectrograms, the observation and analysis of stellar spectra makes an excellent subject for a project.

However, it is possible to construct a very simple spectroscope of your own. All you need is a diffraction grating, a small box such as a shoe box, two razor blades, and some tape. Very inexpensive diffraction gratings (they are actually replicas of gratings on film) can be purchased from supply houses such as Edmund Scientific Company in New Jersey.

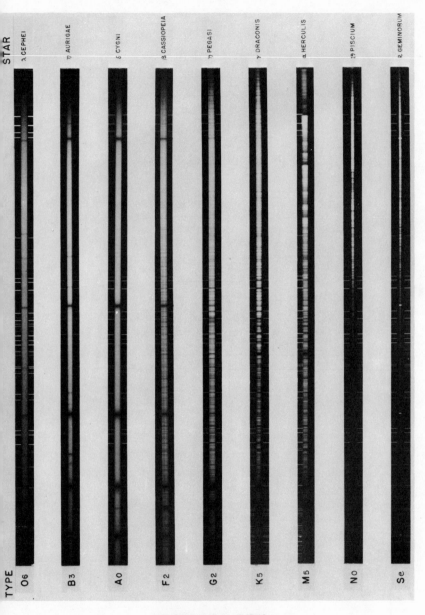

**THE PRINCIPAL TYPES
OF STELLAR SPECTRA**

A Simple Spectroscope

Diffraction grating covering round holes; be sure grating lines run in same direction as slit on opposite side

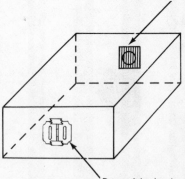

Razor blades taped over slit cut in box to narrow and sharpen opening.

Cut a small, round hole in one end of the box. It should be smaller than the grating's area. On the other end of the box, directly opposite the hole, cut a long, narrow, vertical slit. Use a razor blade to make it no more than ¼ inch (0.625 cm) wide.

Tape the grating over the round hole, making sure that the fine lines also run vertically. To protect the grating, you can cover it with some clear plastic wrap or thin panes of glass. Take the two razor blades and tape them over the vertical slit so that the opening is only 1 millimeter wide. You want a very narrow slit with very sharp edges. Seal the top on the box so that no extraneous light can get in.

Point the slit end of the box at various light sources, and look through the grating. You should see a color fringe on each side of the slit. If the colors appear only at the ends of the slit, the grating must be turned around 90°.

What differences do you find between a fluorescent lamp, a neon sign, and an incandescent lamp? Do not look directly at the sun, but aim the spectroscope off to one side or look at the sky on a cloudy day. You can also look at an open flame from a candle or a stove. Sprinkle salt, baking powder, or other chemical salts over the flame and then observe their spectra.* Find out which elements are in each chemical substance you use, and record what you see through your spectroscope.

This, of course, is a very elementary spectroscope. You cannot observe stellar spectra with it. For that you need a more sophisticated piece of equipment that is usually found in professional observatories. However, there are spectroscopes that can be purchased from places such as Edmund Scientific, but they are rather expensive.

---

*Before you put *any* chemical over a flame, be sure to investigate the reaction that will occur when the substance is heated. Some reactions may be explosive or present a fire hazard.

5

BUILDING A PLANETARIUM

A planetarium is an instrument that is capable of projecting a replica of the heavens on an indoor dome. It can refer either to the projection device itself or to the structure that houses the device. Although professional planetaria are very large and can house hundreds of people, it is possible to build a smaller version.

The dome for a small planetarium can be constructed with cardboard sides and a masonite circular top (masonite or some other stiff material is necessary if you plan to hang the dome from the ceiling). Or you can use thin plywood throughout and have the structure sit on the floor. Of course, an entranceway, covered with cloth, must then be provided.

Use opaque tape on the inside seams to make them as smooth as possible and to seal any light leaks completely. Then paint the inside of the dome with a flat white paint.

The projection apparatus can be a bright bulb shining within a hollow ball. Holes must be carefully drilled into the ball to represent the stars. Different size holes will result in "stars" of different magnitudes. A globe upon which the stars and constellations are depicted can be a great help in positioning the holes correctly. You may even be able to use the globe itself if you can drill neat holes into the material.

THE ZEISS PLANETARIUM
PROJECTOR AT THE
ADLER PLANETARIUM IN
CHICAGO, ILLINOIS

To make the stars rise and set, the instrument must be able to rotate. If you can motorize this action with a variable speed, your planetarium will be easier to operate. This and other effects can be controlled from a circuit board that you can operate during your sky show.

You will want to point out various stars during your show with a flashlight "pointer." To make such a device, attach a cardboard stencil of an arrow to the glass circle on a bright flashlight. Blacken the uncovered area with paint. Remove the stencil. You may have to apply several layers of paint before it is opaque.

If your school already has a planetarium, you may want to construct an addition to it with the use of slides for slide projectors. For example, you can make a set of slides that show the "X-ray sky" or where clusters of galaxies are located in the sky.

One of the simplest types of planetaria requires only a large black umbrella. By positioning the North Star (Polaris) next to the center on the inside, you can then work downward from there, marking first the positions of the stars in the polar constellations. Once the positions are marked, white or colored stars can be pasted in place and dotted lines painted to join the stars in a given constellation.

By tilting the umbrella so that it corresponds to the night sky at your latitude, you can then rotate it and simulate the rising and setting of the stars. This will also demonstrate how the polar stars revolve around the North Star each night. If you support the umbrella behind a desk or table so that part of it is hidden by the furniture, it will give a more realistic appearance to the motions of the stars.

THE ANDROMEDA GALAXY,
WITH TWO SATELLITE GALAXIES
ON EITHER SIDE OF IT

6

MODEL CONSTRUCTION

THE MILKY WAY

You can investigate the spiral structure of our galaxy, the Milky Way, by constructing a three-dimensional model of it. For this you will need a catalog that gives data for galactic star clusters, globular star clusters, H II regions, O-associations, nebulae, and stars. It may be necessary to consult more than one catalog to find information about all of these astronomical objects and regions.

You will need to know the galactic longitude and latitude for each object as well as its distance from us and from the center of the galaxy. This may require some calculations, since catalogs don't always give the exact numbers you need.

For the stars, you will especially need to know about the hot, blue, O-type stars, which are mainly found in the spiral arms. You can use some cool, red, M-type stars as comparison objects, since these are found in other regions.

Most catalogs of celestial objects do not give any data for the H I regions because the stars there are not detectable with optical telescopes. For this data you will have to write to radio observatories. The radio astronomy observatories at Leyden, the Netherlands, and Sydney, Australia, have been especially active in the study of galactic structure and may be able to provide you with information about 21-cm radio observations of H I regions of the Milky Way.

OUR PLACE IN SPACE

Star charts are usually two-dimensional, showing us how the sky appears at night throughout the year. But although the stars appear to be at the same distance from us, we know that their actual distances vary greatly. A three-dimensional star chart is needed to show their true positions in space, relative to the sun.

To construct a three-dimensional star chart of the sun's neighborhood, you will need an up-to-date list of the nearby stars. How far you want to go into space will depend upon how big your model is and what scale you use. You must know each star's right ascension, declination, absolute magnitude, distance from us, and spectral type. Most star catalogs will give this information. A globe upon which the constellations are displayed may also be of help.

Small beads of different sizes and colors can be used to represent the stars. By hanging them from a sturdy board, using different lengths of thin wire or strong thread, you can arrange them around the central "sun" according to their distances from us.

Each star's right ascension and declination will determine on which side of the model sun it should hang as well as how far above or below the sun's level it should be. A large protractor with clearly marked degrees will help you position each bead correctly. Because right ascension is measured in hours rather than in degrees, you must first convert each star's right ascension to degrees or mark off the "hours" on your protractor. One hour equals 15° on a circle.

You may find it necessary to anchor the other end of the wire or thread to a bottom board so that the beads stay in place. Four corner posts between the bottom and top boards will allow you to view the display from all sides and keep it sturdy and rigid.

With such a construction project, you can show why we see certain constellations at different times of the year. You can also show how the sun would appear in the sky if viewed from some other vantage point than the earth. In what constellation, for example, would the sun appear if viewed from Alpha Centauri? From Sirius?

The same type of model can be made for the Local Group of galaxies or for the clusters of galaxies that make up the Local Supercluster.

STELLAR STRUCTURE:
A MODEL STAR

To construct a model of a star, astronomers do not use beads or styrofoam or any other building material. They use mathematical formulae and high-speed computers. Before the age of computers, such a project took over a year to complete and was frequently used as a topic for a Ph.D. dissertation. Now, however, the calculations can be done in minutes. Nevertheless, such a project is still an advanced activity and requires a good command of mathematics.

The sun and most other stars are reasonably stable. They are neither expanding nor contracting, nor does their energy output vary significantly. Such stars are said to be in a state of "equilibrium." All the forces within them are balanced so that at each point within the star the temperature, pressure, and density are maintained at constant values. This condition of equilibrium within a stable star enables us to learn about its internal structure.

The aim of an investigation of the internal structure of a star is to determine the density, temperature, pressure, and chemical composition existing at each point in the stellar interior. The data describing the structure must, at

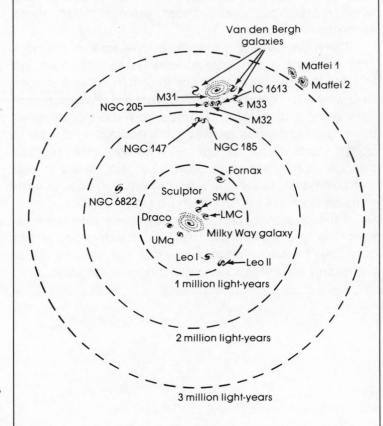

The Local Group of Galaxies

Van den Bergh galaxies

Maffei 1

Maffei 2

M31

IC 1613

NGC 205

M33

M32

NGC 147

NGC 185

Fornax

Sculptor

SMC

NGC 6822

LMC

Draco

Milky Way galaxy

UMa

Leo I

Leo II

1 million light-years

2 million light-years

3 million light-years

THE LOCAL GROUP CONSISTS OF
NEARLY TWO DOZEN KNOWN GALAXIES,
LOCATED WITHIN 3.6 MILLION
LIGHT-YEARS OF THE MILKY WAY.

the same time, satisfy a number of equations that relate to them. Thus, investigations of stellar structure require the construction, by mathematical calculations, of a synthetic gaseous model that satisfies known physical laws and whose mass, radius, and luminosity are matched to those of the observed star.

There are several methods to formulate mathematically the physical principles governing stellar structure and to solve the resulting equations to obtain a stellar model. One way is to describe quantitatively the physical conditions existing at a given distance from the star's center. Using these chosen quantities in the equations referred to above, one must determine whether their gradual change as the reference point is moved inward or outward ultimately allows them to agree with measurements of these quantities in an observed star.

If the chosen quantities do not agree with observations, the researcher must start again with a new set of quantities for each variable. You can see why the use of computers has been such a great help in this work.

7

OBSERVING
THE SUN

The face of the sun is constantly changing, and therefore, observation of this "daytime star" is always challenging. And it is the one astronomical object for which lack of light is never a problem, especially when photography is being considered. In fact, the overabundance of light and heat are the real problems in solar observations.

Because the powerful rays from the sun are very dangerous if viewed directly, other methods must be used. There are all kinds of devices that can be attached to your telescope to allow relatively safe solar viewing, but perhaps the best and safest method is by projection.

The solar image, after being magnified by the eyepiece in your telescope, is projected onto a white screen. How far the screen should be from the eyepiece is determined by trial and error. Then the screen is attached to the telescope to hold it steady at the optimum distance.

You will also find that a sunshield will be necessary to shade the white screen so that only the projected image shines on it directly. A large piece of stiff cardboard or thin plywood with a hole large enough to slip over the telescope tube may suffice. Or you may want to construct a projection box so that even more extraneous light is kept out. You may have made such projection boxes to observe solar eclipses. Now, however, the box is attached to the telescope.

Once you have attached the screen and shield or projection box to your telescope, you can start observing the solar surface safely. You will note on the screen some dark spots when the solar image is projected. These are sunspots. They will change their shapes and positions day by day. These changes can be easily recorded by observing them every sunny day.

First, determine how large your projected sun appears on your screen (a 6-inch (15-cm) diameter will give you enough room for detail). Make a circle of that size on a piece of white cardboard and cover the circle with grid lines about ½ inch (1.25 cm) apart. All of these lines should be dark enough to be seen through thin white paper.

Use a new sheet of thin paper for each observation. On each sheet draw a circle the same size as the one on the cardboard. Leave room on the paper for other data such as the date, time, conditions of seeing, etc. You may also want to indicate the compass points on the circle— north at the top, south at the bottom, east to the right, and west to the left (a mirror image of the real sun). The recording of the time can be in Universal Time (U.T.) or local time, but be sure to state which time standard you are using.

For each daily observation, a sheet of marked white paper is clipped onto the cardboard so that the circles match. The grid on the cardboard will help you position the spots more easily.

Carefully trace each projected sunspot on the white circle. If you have no telescope clock drive, the projected

THE ENTIRE DISK OF THE SUN AND AN ENLARGED VIEW OF AN UNUSUALLY BIG SUNSPOT GROUP

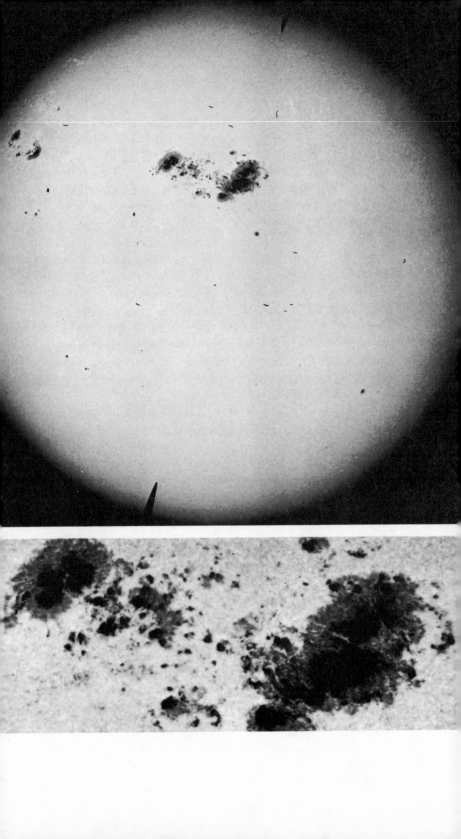

image will drift from right to left as the sun moves in the sky. For this reason, an equatorial stand with a clock drive is a great help. Otherwise, you must manually bring the image back to the circle on the paper before tracing the next spot's position.

Individual spots and groups of spots will change in appearance from day to day. They will also travel across the sun's surface from right to left. This, of course, is due to the sun's rotation.

You may want to concentrate on the changing appearance of one or more groups of sunspots rather than recording their positions and numbers. This requires good artistic ability as well as patience and experience, since accurate reproduction of the finer details of the umbra and penumbra are necessary. A 6-inch (15-cm) telescope is the smallest aperture possible for this work to be of value. One method includes making serial drawings of the sunspots, with time intervals determined by how rapidly the visible changes are occurring.

A study of the rate of growth and decay of sunspots and any possible correlation between this rate and the sunspot types, their latitudes, the phases of the sunspot cycle, and so on, can be undertaken. Such a study does not require a large telescope. Find out if there is a correlation between the longitudinal distribution of sunspots and their sizes, longevity, type, or the phase of the sunspot cycle.

Is there a correlation between visual solar phenomena (sunspots and flares) and solar radio radiation output? Does solar variability affect terrestrial weather conditions such as rainfall and temperature? What is the relationship between sunspot activity and the chromospheric disturbances above them (flares, prominences, etc.)? How big are the sunspots you have observed? Can you calculate the sun's rotational velocity from your observations?

It is very important that you consult recent literature

for solar references and research. There has been a great deal of solar research in the last ten to fifteen years. In the literature, other observing projects will be found or will suggest themselves to you.

PHOTOGRAPHING THE SUN

Because of the superabundance of light, short exposures of the sun, with no guiding of the telescope necessary, become possible. You can use slow, fine-grain emulsions and take the time to select moments when the seeing is ideal. The size of the aperture is important only for resolution.

Photograph a continuous record of sunspot detail and growth and decay. Record the changes of active groups of sunspots at frequent intervals. Such photographs make an excellent addition to any project display or can become the project itself if done thoroughly. Once again, correlations between changes in the sunspots and their size, longevity, position, and phase of the cycle should be studied as part of the project.

Solar eclipses offer another great photographic opportunity. Even partial eclipses can be recorded, although these are not as important as total solar eclipses. A photographic record of the progress of the moon as it covers the solar disk and then moves off it again should be accompanied by other observations of the eclipse. Changes in temperature, shadow effects, and animal behavior are just some of the things to notice and record.

SPECTROSCOPIC OBSERVATION OF THE SUN

You don't need very sophisticated equipment to see the main features of the Fraunhofer spectrum, but for any real study, a minimum amount of dispersion and aperture are needed. Your telescope aperture should be at least 4 inches (10 cm), and 6 inches (15 cm) would be even better. You should be able to separate clearly the D_1 and D_2 lines (sodium) in the yellow part of the spectrum for serious work.

Spectra can be obtained of flares, sunspots, prominences, or any other feature on the solar surface. To observe flares, you really need a spectrohelioscope, which may be too advanced a piece of equipment for most amateur astronomers.

As for prominences, normally the brilliant glare of the sun prevents us from seeing these huge tongues of flame that appear to leap out from the solar limb. But there are instruments that obscure the main disk of the sun and block out much of the scattered light surrounding it. Then only the limb—and the prominences that leap above it—are visible. There are special solar spectroscopes for viewing prominences, and there are also prominence telescopes constructed for this purpose. It is possible to make a prominence telescope inexpensively, but you need special equipment to do the necessary precision work.

THE SUN'S RADIATION

How much radiation do we receive from the sun? We can measure the amount of heat the sun gives us with the use of a pyrheliometer. This is an instrument that measures the increase in the temperature of a solid or liquid exposed to sunlight for a given length of time. It is actually a form of a radiometer used to measure solar energy. (A radiometer measures heat intensity, i.e., the amount of heat radiation received by an object on the earth.)

With a pyrheliometer you can calculate the "solar constant." This is the amount of energy from the sun that falls on 1 square centimeter of the earth. You must be sure first that all the heat measured by the pyrheliometer is coming from the sun, and that none is lost during the experiment. The professional measurement of the solar constant is the quantity of energy received per cm^2 just outside the earth's atmosphere, but your measurement will be close to this amount.

Once the solar constant has been determined, the sun's total energy output can be calculated. Imagine a huge sphere around the sun, with a diameter equal to the earth's orbit. The earth in its orbit lies on this sphere. What is the surface area of this imaginary sphere?

If you multiply this area (in cm^2 units) by your measure of the solar constant, you should arrive at a total solar output of approximately 4×10^{33} ergs/sec. Can you relate this amount of energy to a light bulb or automobile engine output? What percentage of this solar energy does the earth receive?

8

OBSERVING THE MOON

Projects involving the moon are numerous. The moon is probably the most observed celestial body. You can investigate the lunar phases or perhaps a lunar eclipse. You can study the moon's surface features or its motion through the sky. Or you can use the moon to study the occultations of stars.

You probably remember projects in elementary school that explained the phases of the moon. But now you can investigate whether the lunar phases have any effect on the earth. Is there any correlation between the phases of the moon and the amount of precipitation on earth? Do plants grow better if planted during a specific phase? Are there more crimes committed at full moon or at some other phase?

For another project, observe the moon in its path through the stars. Plot each observation, and make a drawing of the lunar phase on that date. Record the date, time, comparison stars used, and the angular distance of the moon from these stars. Estimate the right ascension and declination of the moon at each observation. Then plot the moon's observed position on a star chart that shows the celestial equator and the ecliptic. Estimate the inclination of the moon's orbit to the ecliptic and the celestial equator. Do you notice any change in the moon's orbit from month to month? From your observations, estimate the moon's sidereal and synodic periods.

THROUGH A TELESCOPE, THE MOON (AND EVERYTHING
ELSE) APPEARS INVERTED, OR UPSIDE DOWN.
HOWEVER, LIKE HERE, IT IS USUALLY SHOWN AS IT
APPEARS TO THE NAKED EYE, WITH "NORTH" AT THE TOP.

In conjunction with these observations, record the times of lunar risings and settings. What is the average time difference of moonrise on successive nights? Why does this time vary throughout the year? What is meant by the expression "The moon rides high in winter."? What is the relationship between the lunar phase and the moon's position in the sky at any given time? With the use of photographs, charts, and diagrams, answer the above questions.

THE LUNAR ECLIPSE

The path of the moon around the earth (the lunar orbit) intersects the apparent path of the sun through the sky (the ecliptic). A movable three-dimensional exhibit can be constructed that shows these two great circles at a small angle to each other. On such a model, the nodes can be labeled and their regression demonstrated. With your model you can explain why we don't have eclipses every new or full moon. What is the Saros cycle? From a list of previous solar and lunar eclipses, can you predict future ones? How?

There will be no more total solar eclipses visible from the continental United States in this century, but there will be a few partial eclipses as well as many lunar eclipses. Plan to observe such an eclipse and to photograph it. For solar eclipses, even for partial ones, a special solar observational setup will be necessary (see Chapter Seven).

To photograph a lunar eclipse, a 35mm camera loaded with high-speed film is ideal. Before the eclipse starts, when the full moon is at its brightest, your exposures should be about 1/500 to 1/250 of a second at f/11. Longer exposures will be necessary as the moon darkens while it enters the earth's shadow.

A sturdy tripod and a long cable release should be used to avoid jarring the camera. This is especially important if you use a telephoto lens, since any camera motion is magnified as much as the image itself. A 200mm lens with a 2× tele-extender should give good results.

Of course, if you have your camera attached to a telescope, that is even better. Then the camera lens is removed, and the telescope's optical system becomes the photographic lens.

Cameras with double-exposure capability can be used to produce a sequence photograph. Use a low-power telephoto lens (or your telescope lens), and position the moon first in the lower left-hand corner of the viewfinder screen. As the moon darkens, move the camera one lunar diameter after each exposure. In that way, you can capture the entire eclipse on a single frame.

The moon moves the distance of its own diameter every hour. You may be able to position the camera so that the moon will move across the viewfinder's field without your having to move the camera. This will, of course, limit the number of exposures you can take, unless you want them to overlap.

THE MOON ILLUSION

You have probably noticed how large the full moon appears when it is rising. Six hours later, when it is overhead, it appears much smaller. Many theories have been suggested to explain this phenomenon. Make a series of photographs of the rising moon and compare sizes. If you have a camera that allows double exposures, you can make a series of exposures on a single frame, as you did for the lunar eclipse series. What does the camera reveal? Can you explain this phenomenon?

THE LUNAR SURFACE

A three-dimensional moonscape can be made by sculpting the various features out of clay or some other material such as plaster of Paris. You can either choose a small region to display or use a globe and depict the entire lunar surface. Use a material that can be painted so that the maria and highlands will stand out clearly. Photographs taken by the Apollo astronauts as well as earlier space probes should be used for guidance. You can show, with the use of a bright flashlight, the way the various features appear during different phases of the moon.

CRATERING

All of the solid bodies of the solar system, including the earth, show evidence of cratering from their distant past. Craters are most noticeable on those bodies that have no erosive element such as wind or water. Obvious examples are the moon and Mercury.

Most of these craters are believed to have formed when meteorites hit the surfaces of the moons and planets. This happened billions of years ago, in the very early history of the solar system. Practically all of the large rocks and debris are gone now from interplanetary space, and therefore new craters of any appreciable size are extremely rare events.

You can simulate crater formation easily by pelting wet sand or dirt with various-size rocks and stones. Throw the stones into the soil with different amounts of force. Vary the angle of impact. Try it when the soil is very dry or very wet. Can you create a crater with a peak at its center? Take photographs of your craters, and compare them with those taken of the moon or Mercury.

Make a small model of a crater by throwing a stone into partially hardened plaster of Paris or cement or some other material that will hold the "crater" shape when it dries and hardens. The small model can be displayed in your exhibit. If you use small aluminum throwaway baking pans, you will be able to display several different craters along with your photographs.

THE LUNAR TERRAIN. NOTE THE PEAKS
IN THE CENTER OF THE LARGE CRATER
IN THE UPPER LEFT-HAND CORNER AND
THE MANY TINY CRATERS THAT HAVE
POCKMARKED THE ENTIRE SURFACE.

THE SURFACE OF MERCURY,
PHOTOGRAPHED BY *MARINER 10*

What is the relationship between the force of impact and the size of the crater? the depth of the crater? How does the size of the stone affect the shape and size of the crater? How does the angle of impact affect the shape and size of the crater? What other variables affect cratering?

Some craters are believed to have been formed by volcanic activity rather than by meteorites. To simulate this kind of crater, bury the end of a plastic hose in dry sand so that the opening points upward. There should be about 3 inches (7.5 cm) of sand over the hose. Blow very hard through the other end of the hose (or use an air pump). How are volcanic craters similar or dissimilar to the meteoritic ones?

9

OBSERVING THE PLANETS

Observing the planets is probably one of the favorite activities in astronomy for those with modest equipment. But to be of any value, the observations must be done with great accuracy and attention to detail. In terms of observing, each planet has its own limitations that must be understood before any project is started. Here, briefly, are some of the possible activities that can be undertaken. With more professional equipment, of course, much more advanced work can be done.

Mercury is a difficult object to see because it is always so close to the sun in the sky. However, if you have a good vantage point from which to observe, you can use the same suggested projects for Mercury as for Venus.

In addition to those projects, you may be interested in observing a very important event that will occur on November 13, 1986. Mercury will make a transit across the face of the sun. There will be only two more transits this century, so the 1986 event will be watched and recorded by many amateur and professional astronomers. If you have prepared your telescope to observe the solar surface as suggested in Chapter Seven, you will also be able to observe and possibly photograph the transit. Be sure to record the exact time that Mercury's disk is seen on the projected solar disk. Drawings and/or photographs should be included in your report.

Venus is probably the easiest planet to see because it gets so very bright, reaching -4 magnitude at times. Its path can be plotted through the stars over a period of several months, using a star chart for guidance. Diagrams can be drawn showing Venus' position relative to the earth and sun for each observation. If a telescope is available, make drawings of Venus as seen through the telescope at various times. You will note that it goes through phases similar to the moon. However, we never see all of Venus' phases. An explanation with diagrams of this phenomenon should accompany your report. Galileo, who first discovered that Venus has phases like the moon, had a very unique way of announcing his discovery: "The mother of love imitates Diana." Can you explain such a statement? Galileo's discovery was perhaps one of the most important ones that he made with his very small telescopes. Galileo did not have a camera to take pictures of his findings, but if you can photograph Venus' phases, the pictures would be a good addition to your project.

Mars is another planet that is easy to find and to follow through the sky. If you plot its path over a period of several months, try to pick a time when it exhibits retrograde motion. Then use diagrams to explain this seemingly backward motion and explain how ancient astronomers such as Ptolemy explained it. You will find other projects involving Mars later on in this chapter.

Jupiter provides a variety of phenomena to observe. Because it moves quite slowly through the stars, plotting its path has to be done over a period of at least six months to show any real movement. Jupiter also exhibits retrograde motion and can be used in a similar manner as was suggested for Mars.

Jupiter's angular size and its brightness allows small telescopes to be used for observing its colorful clouds. If your telescope is big enough, you can make drawings or take photographs of this planet (assuming that the camera is attached to the telescope) to show changes in the

VENUS AS PHOTOGRAPHED BY *MARINER 10.*
BOTH THE DARK AND LIGHT AREAS ARE
THICK CLOUDS COVERING THE PLANET'S SURFACE.

The Phases of Venus

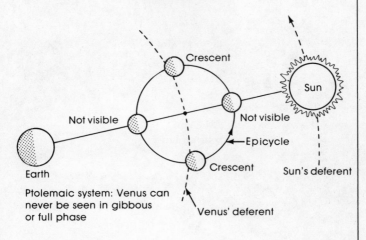

Crescent

Sun

Not visible

Not visible

Epicycle

Earth

Crescent

Sun's deferent

Ptolemaic system: Venus can never be seen in gibbous or full phase

Venus' deferent

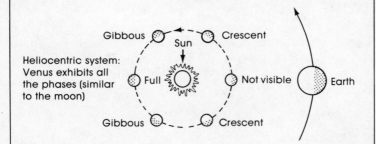

Gibbous

Crescent

Sun

Heliocentric system: Venus exhibits all the phases (similar to the moon)

Full

Not visible

Earth

Gibbous

Crescent

THE GIANT PLANET JUPITER,
AS PHOTOGRAPHED BY *PIONEER 10*

bands and in the position of the Great Red Spot and other turbulent areas.

Even a very small telescope or pair of binoculars will reveal the four largest Jovian moons. A study of their transits and occultations can be made as well as determining their rates of revolution. Such a project is described later in this chapter.

Saturn can also be followed through the stars, although its motion is even slower than Jupiter's. Most small telescopes will allow you to see Saturn's ring system as well as its colorful bands. Usually, however, not enough detail will be distinguished to make any real study possible.

The asteroids can be tracked down and identified, and the brighter ones can be photographed. But otherwise, there is very little study or observation here for the amateur astronomer. New discoveries are made today by photography, and it is doubtful that any more bright asteroids remain to be detected. However, if you want to try to find the known ones, there are about twenty-five that are brighter than magnitude +10. They usually appear yellowish and are very starlike in appearance in small telescopes.

You can detect asteroids photographically by guiding your telescope on a star in the asteroid's vicinity. The star will remain a point of light, while the asteroid makes a trail on the photograph. Focusing on any star near the ecliptic for several hours with a wide-angle lens will eventually reveal asteroid trails. Or you can use the "Blink Method" described in Chapter Sixteen.

The Blink Method can also be used to detect the outermost planets, Uranus, Neptune, and Pluto. But there is very little else you can do in the way of research on these very distant bodies.

Although the big "Jupiter effect" scare of 1981 has passed without incident, many researchers are still trying to determine if the planetary positions ever have any

THE PLANET SATURN, AS SEEN FROM EARTH
THROUGH A 61-INCH (15.5-M) TELESCOPE

effect on solar or geological activity. You can try to determine if any such correlation exists by reviewing the pattern of solar or terrestrial earthquake activity (or other natural events) and then comparing these events with the planetary positions at that time. You might also compare astrological predictions with these events.

To study the solar system as a whole entity, you can start by constructing a model of it. This can be done with construction toys or with different-size styrofoam balls hanging from sticks of the appropriate length. Use an electric light bulb at the center to represent the sun. Because of the great distances of the outer planets from the sun as compared with the inner planets, you probably won't be able to include more than the orbit of Saturn in your model. Using a variable-speed electric motor you can make the planet models revolve and possibly rotate as well. Can you add the larger moons to this exhibit and have them revolve around their respective planets?

Along with such a model you may also want to make a chart of the planets showing such information as distance from the sun, eccentricity of orbit, period of revolution, orbital velocity, period of rotation, inclination of the equator to the orbital plane, diameter, volume, mass, surface gravity, density, escape velocity, surface features, atmospheric composition and features, atmospheric pressure at the surface, temperature at the surface and at the cloudtops (if any), the amount of sunlight received, moons, rings, and so on. In many cases you will want to give the quantity in comparison to the earth (earth = 1) rather than the absolute quantity.

THE MARTIAN "RIVERBEDS"

The Viking and Mariner missions to Mars revealed many features that were quite surprising. Photographs of the Martian terrain showed none of the legendary canals but did suggest the strong possibility of running water sometime in the distant past. There is no liquid water now, although the ice caps are partially composed of frozen water, and the soil and rocks have water in them.

Using photographs from the Viking or Mariner missions, compare them with similar terrestrial conditions such as dried riverbeds. What similarities or differences do you see?

You can create a model of a riverbed with sand or dirt. For this you will need a large area such as a standard sandbox. Place it in a bright, sunny place so that it will dry quickly and be easy to photograph. Later, you will want to make a smaller model for your display.

Using a garden hose with a variable nozzle, run water in a stream over the surface of the sand. In order to have your "river" flow, you may have to tilt the box slightly. Vary the force and amount of water in the stream or the width of the stream itself. Put different-size rocks in the path of the stream. Bury some of the rocks in the sand or dirt before letting the water flow over it.

Let the water drain out of the sand before photographing the path that it made. Then smooth out the sand for the next trial stream. Compare your photographs with those taken by the Viking probes and with pictures of dried riverbeds here on earth. Were you able to create any "channel islands" or "river deltas"?

If you cannot create the same effects in a smaller model, try recreating some of the ones from your sandbox by modeling them in clay or plaster of Paris or papiermâché.

A MARTIAN LANDSCAPE.
THIS PHOTOMOSAIC SHOWS
CHANNELS THAT RESEMBLE
DRIED RIVERBEDS ON
EARTH. ALSO NOTE THE
CRATERS ON THE SURFACE.

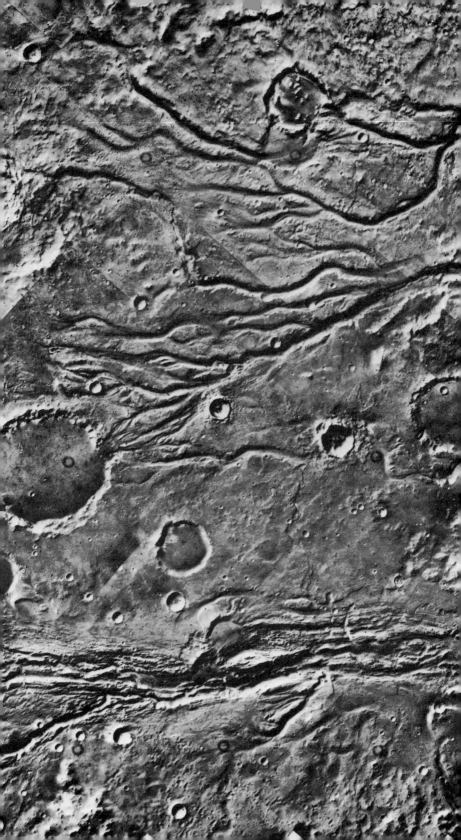

THOSE MYSTERIOUS CANALS OF MARS

In 1879, Giovanni Schiaparelli, an Italian astronomer, published a map of Mars that he had drawn from his observations of the planet through a telescope. On the map were a series of interlacing lines that he called *canali*, the Italian word for "channels." Unfortunately, the word was mistranslated into English as "canals," and the assumption was made that if canals exist on Mars, intelligent life must exist there also.

The controversy that ensued regarding life on Mars was not settled until the *Mariner 9* space probe orbited Mars in 1971–72. It photographed nearly the entire Martian surface and found no canals. The hundreds of channels on Mars are all too small to have been observed from earth.

How could Schiaparelli and so many other nineteenth-century observers have made so big a mistake? What did they see? Certainly the power of suggestion that the canals were there must have made many of the later observers think they were seeing them.

To illustrate this, select an abstract painting (or draw one yourself), and let others look at it from a distance (or perhaps through a long tube to simulate looking through a telescope). Ask each person to sketch what he or she sees. Allow only a few minutes for this. And to see what the power of suggestion can do, casually comment that the last person who viewed the scene thought it was a house or a cat or whatever the drawing might possibly look like. If you use an important name, such as the name of your principal or of the mayor of your town, the effect may be greater. Compare what those subjects who were "prompted" drew with drawings by people who were not given suggestions.

Although this is not strictly a project in astronomy, it does reveal some of the problems inherent in observational astronomy and in achieving a truly scientific result in any experiment.

THE MOONS OF JUPITER

The four largest Jovian moons can be seen very easily through a small telescope or even through a pair of binoculars. In fact, some of them would be bright enough to be visible to the naked eye if the overpowering brilliance of Jupiter could be eliminated.

Each moon revolves around the planet in its own orbit, with a very regular period of revolution. By careful observation of each moon as it changes its position hour by hour and day by day, these periods can be determined.

Through the telescope you will see a bright disk (Jupiter) and up to four smaller disks, all more or less in a row. They may not all be on the same side of Jupiter. If less than four are visible, the others may either be on the far side of Jupiter or in front of it. A large telescope is needed to detect a transiting moon or the shadow it makes on the Jovian clouds. But with experience, you will be able to determine when each moon is being eclipsed or is transiting the planet.

Observations should be made at least once every evening, weather permitting. You may want to make more than one observation per night until you are more familiar with each moon's motion and can easily distinguish one from another. Allow at least several hours to elapse between each observation.

Each time you make an observation, draw a small diagram showing where each moon is, relative to Jupiter. Graph paper will help you place the moons more accurately. Indicate the date and time of your observations. Once you have made enough observations, you should be able to determine which moon is which in each diagram and to estimate each moon's period of revolution. An example of how your diagrams might look is given on page 64.

This project requires very little observing time, but accuracy is very important. The more observations you are able to make, the better your conclusions will be.

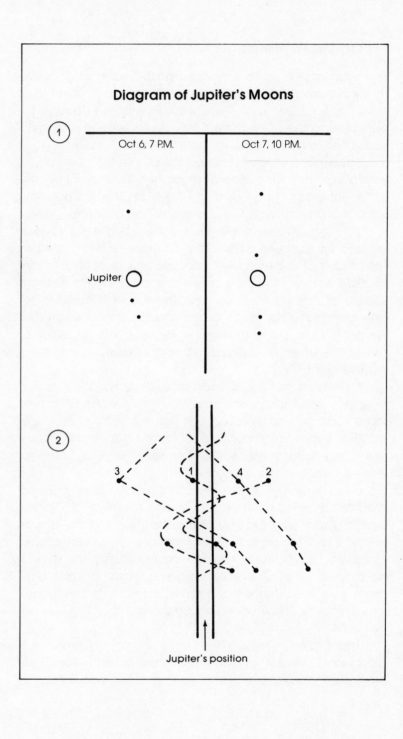

Diagram of Jupiter's Moons

① Oct 6, 7 P.M.   Oct 7, 10 P.M.

Jupiter

② 3   1   4   2

Jupiter's position

Once you have determined the periods of revolution and are able to predict when each moon will be eclipsed by Jupiter, you can see how accurate your predictions are. Remember that the distance between the earth and Jupiter is a factor in this timing. You may be able to repeat Olaus Roemer's experiment in which he determined the speed of light by timing the eclipses of Jupiter's moons.

THE EARTH AS VIEWED FROM SPACE
BY THE *APOLLO 11* ASTRONAUTS

10

MEASURING THE EARTH'S CIRCUMFERENCE

How big is the earth? The famous Egyptian scientist Eratosthenes tried to answer this question more than two thousand years ago.

Eratosthenes knew that in Egypt in the city of Syene (today Aswan), the sun was directly overhead at noon on the first day of summer each year. The bottom of a deep well there was always completely sunlit at that hour. While he was in Alexandria, Egypt, a city to the north of Syene, Eratosthenes found that a stick planted vertically in the ground cast a shadow at noon of that same day, proving that the sun was not overhead there. By using the length of the shadow, the Egyptian scientist was able to measure the angle of the sun from the zenith. It was about 1/50 of a circle, or approximately 7.2°. This angle, he concluded, was equal to the angle at the center of the earth made by the distance between the two cities. Once he had measured this distance accurately, he could determine the total circumference of the earth by multiplying this amount by 50.

Eratosthenes didn't use the same units of measurement as we do today, but by converting his units to ours, we find that his measurements gave an answer of about 24,385 miles (39,016 km). Considering the simple tools he used, his results were very accurate.

Of course, today we have much more accurate

methods of determining the circumference of the earth, but it is possible to repeat Eratosthenes' experiment. See if you can come as close as he did to the true answer.

You will need the help of another person living a few hundred miles to the north or south of you (unless you want to wait a full year and then travel north or south to do your own measuring on exactly the same day of the year). Each of you must take your measurements on the same day at local noon. This is when the sun is highest in the sky for that day. However, local noon may not agree with your clock's noon, so you (and your fellow measurer) must determine when local noon actually occurs, i.e., noon according to the "apparent solar time."

To determine the exact time of local noon, you will need a long, straight, thin stick and a much shorter, straight stick. Plant the long stick vertically into the ground. Make sure that it is exactly upright by using a plumb line or a carpenter's level. Plant the shorter stick into the ground directly north of the long stick about 20 inches (50 cm) away. The north direction can be determined with a compass.*

When the shadow of the long stick touches the short stick, the time is local noon. The sun is at its highest point in the sky for that day. You have made a very simple sundial.

Now you must measure the angle of the sun from the zenith point. This requires the construction of a "solar quadrant." For this you will need a straight stick of wood about 1½ feet (45 cm) long, a large half-circle protractor with degrees and half-degrees marked clearly, and a large nail.

Attach the protractor along the upper part of the stick so that half of it rises above the end of the stick. Drive

* Because a compass needle does not point to the North Pole but rather to the North Magnetic Pole, at night compare the needle's direction with that of the North Star (Polaris). This difference will be found to be quite small unless you are very far north.

Eratosthenes' Experiment

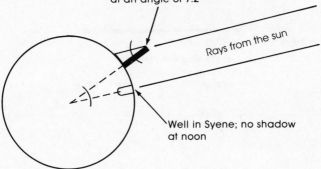

Tower in Alexandria casts shadow
at an angle of 7.2°

Rays from the sun

Well in Syene; no shadow
at noon

7.2° = 1/50 of a circle

Determining Local Noon

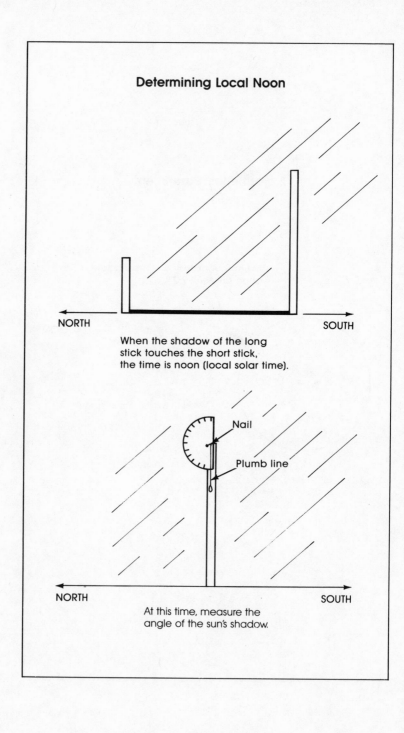

NORTH SOUTH

When the shadow of the long
stick touches the short stick,
the time is noon (local solar time).

Nail

Plumb line

NORTH SOUTH

At this time, measure the
angle of the sun's shadow.

the nail into the stick, through the protractor, at the middle of the straight edge. See the diagram on page 70.

Place the stick in the ground vertically near your sundial. Turn it so that the protractor lies in the north-south direction. Again use a plumb line or level to make sure that it is exactly vertical. Use a compass to determine the north-south orientation.

When your sundial tells you it is local noon, note where the shadow of the nail falls on the protractor. Record this angle as precisely as possible. Be sure to record the date as well.

You must now determine exactly how far away your fellow measurer is. You should consider the north-south distance only. If you are not exactly north or south of each other (few places are), you cannot use the given map distances but will have to make some calculations. You may be able to use the scale on a large map to measure this amount. With this information and the difference between the angles you both measured, you should be able to roughly determine the circumference of the earth.

WHY AREN'T PLANETS SPHERICAL?

In the above experiment, you were measuring the circumference of the earth around the poles. This is not the same distance as the earth's equator because the earth is not a sphere. It is an oblate spheroid; that is, it is slightly flattened at the poles. The larger planets are even less spherical than the earth. This is because they rotate even faster.

You can investigate the relationship between rotational speed and polar flattening of a rotating body with the use of a rotator, which is usually available in a physics lab. If the rotator already has a metal hoop attached, fine, but a governor from a steam or gasoline engine will work just as well. Or, you can attach a flexible, thin metal hoop to it yourself.

Make a graph of the various speeds and the amount of flattening that takes place. Compare this effect with the rotational speed and the flattening of the earth, Jupiter, and Saturn.

By attaching a flexible loop to it, you may also do this experiment with a power drill that has variable speeds. A hand drill can also be used to demonstrate the effects, although its speed will be more difficult to measure accurately.

11

COMETS AND METEORS

The most spectacular minor members of the solar system are the comets. Observed from earliest times, they were most frequently regarded as omens of disaster. Some early philosophers even held that they were sins of mankind burning as they rose through the atmosphere. It was not until the sixteenth century that astronomers were able to establish that comets were actually distant objects, far outside our planet's atmosphere.

The most famous comet is named after Edmund Halley, an English astronomer who proved that comets were actually members of the solar system and that they revolved around the sun. However, unlike the planets, the orbits of most comets, including Halley's, are very elongated. They travel far out beyond the planets and then come in, passing very close to the sun.

Halley's Comet returns to the inner solar system every seventy-five years. It is due to arrive here again during the winter of 1985–86. Astronomers started looking for it as early as 1977, eight years before it was due to pass perihelion. But at that time it was still as far away as Uranus and was not observable, even through the most powerful telescopes.

During the winter of 1985–86, this famous comet will be easier to see. However, binoculars or small telescopes will probably be needed except under the most ideal

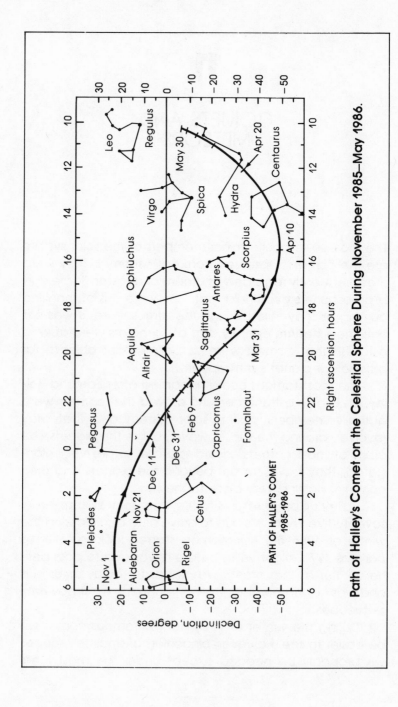

Path of Halley's Comet on the Celestial Sphere During November 1985–May 1986.

viewing conditions. And the successful observer will have to know when and where to look. The general public will probably be disappointed.

The coming of Halley's Comet is a rare opportunity for many amateur astronomers to show their ability to observe, photograph, and record an important astronomical event. To help you locate the comet, the National Aeronautics and Space Administration (NASA) has published a booklet, "The Comet Halley Handbook," by Donald K. Yeomans. If you plan to do a project observing Halley's Comet, this booklet will be of enormous help. There are also several books already on the bookshelves that can give you a lot of information about this and other comets. In addition, the American Museum of Natural History's Hayden Planetarium has a map and a short article about Halley's Comet available to the public.

The photographing of a comet as it approaches and recedes from the sun requires great patience and effort. The cometary image is rather faint, and therefore long time exposures are necessary. You must have a good telescope and camera and be able to track the comet over a period of an hour or more. Actually, you will use the telescope to guide the camera as the comet moves among the stars. The resulting photograph, if done correctly, will show straight star trails in the same field as the comet.

If you have good artistic ability, you can draw careful sketches of the comet as it changes hour by hour or day by day. Visual observations through a telescope are sometimes better than photography because finer details and rapid changes are not always easily recorded photographically.

When viewing the end of the tail, you will want to use very low magnification. And in general you should use the smallest aperture that shows the comet clearly. Some trial and error will be necessary once you are able to sight the comet itself.

All observations, whether visual or photographic, must have the date and time on them as well as the length of the observation and the seeing conditions.

Visual observations can answer the following questions concerning the various features of the comet. These features, of course, apply to any comet, not just Halley's.

Coma. What is its size and shape? Does it have a halo around it? Are there any jets coming out of it?

Nucleus. This is very small and may not be visible at all. If visible, is it single or multiple? Is it a disk or a starlike point?

Tail. How long is it? What is its position relative to the sun? the stars? Is there one or are there several tails, and if several, how long are they and what are their positions? Are there any fluctuations of light along the tail?

A chart should be kept showing the comet's motion through the stars from the earliest point of visibility. The chart should extend over several months. Then, from a series of observations of the comet's position, its orbit can be computed. The calculated orbit will be more precise if many observations are made over a long period of time. Although astronomers have carefully estimated where Halley's orbit will be as it swings around the sun, these figures remain only estimates until the comet is actually sighted in the sky.

Advanced mathematics are necessary to compute the six "elements" that completely define the comet's elliptical orbit and its position at any given time. The use of a computer is of great help in these calculations, although they were done with pencil and paper long before computers were invented.

Once the orbit is computed, a three-dimensional map or chart can be constructed, showing the plane of the

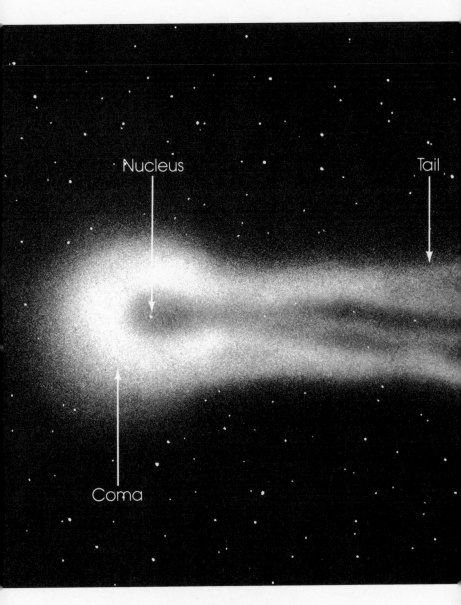

Nucleus

Tail

Coma

PARTS OF A COMET. THE TINY
NUCLEUS AND THE COMA MAKE UP
THE "HEAD" OF THE COMET.

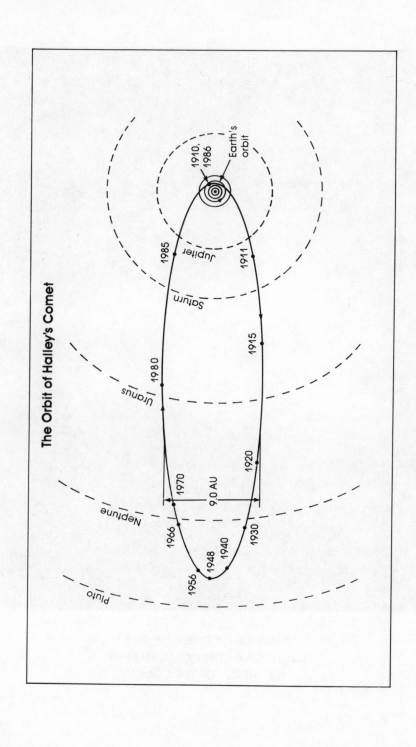

The Orbit of Halley's Comet

comet's orbit and the plane of the ecliptic. The angle formed when these two planes intersect each other is one of the "elements" that must first be worked out. The comet's position on several dates can be indicated on the model.

METEOR SHOWERS

On any dark, clear night you can usually see at least one or two meteors streak across the sky every hour. But if you observe on a night when a meteor shower is due, you may see from fifteen to fifty meteors an hour, and sometimes even more. The number depends upon how concentrated the meteoroid swarm is. Each swarm is associated with a specific comet's orbit; the particles in the swarm are cometary debris left behind as the comet orbits the sun.

When the earth passes through such swarms of cometary debris, the particles enter the earth's atmosphere, burning up by the heat friction they create with the air molecules. The result is a "meteor shower." The meteors, instead of appearing in different parts of the sky, all seem to come from one point, which is called the "radiant." If you carefully plot the meteor trails on a sky chart, you can determine the radiant. Of course, some meteors that night will not be part of the shower and will not radiate from that point in the sky.

The table on the following page gives the names and dates of the major meteor showers. It also tells how many meteors are usually sighted per hour. The names of the showers are derived from the constellations from which the meteors appear to be coming, i.e., the radiant.

To plot meteor paths, you must first be very familiar with the night sky. You should know the constellations very well and be able to identify all visible stars to at least the 3rd or 4th magnitude. A star atlas will be of great assistance here.

MAJOR METEOR SHOWERS

Shower	Date of Maximum Number of Meteors	Hourly Rate for a Single Observer	Position of Radiant R.A. h	Position of Radiant R.A. m	Declination Degrees
Quadrantids	Jan. 3	40	15	28	+50
Lyrids	April 21	15	18	16	+34
η Aquarids	May 4	20	22	24	00
δ Aquarids	July 28	20	22	36	−17
Perseids	Aug. 11	50	03	04	+58
Orionids	Oct. 21	25	06	20	+15
Taurids	Nov. 4	15	03	32	+14
Leonids	Nov. 16	15	10	08	+22
Geminids	Dec. 13	50	07	32	+32
Ursids	Dec. 22	15	14	28	+76

You must also be prepared to observe after midnight. That is when most meteors hit the earth because the after-midnight side of the earth faces the direction in which the earth is moving. And since meteors are not usually very bright, your observing station must be away from any bright lights or polluted air. The middle of a cornfield or some other unsettled area would be suitable.

Remember that such observing will require several hours, so come prepared with adequate clothing, food to munch on, insect repellent (if it's summertime), etc. You will also need star maps on which to draw meteor trails, a reference star chart, a shaded flashlight (or one covered with red cellophane) to avoid destroying your night vision while checking the charts, and an accurate watch to record the time and duration of each meteor flight. The length of time each meteor takes is difficult to measure. Most people think they last a few seconds, whereas most are no more than a fraction of a second in duration.

If simultaneous observations are made about 20 miles (32 km) apart, you can then compute the height of the meteors. Of course, you must know the exact distance between the observing stations. When you compare the two star maps showing the meteor's path, you will find that the paths are parallel to each other. Their separation in degrees is one of the angles of the triangle made by the meteor and the two stations. If the meteor is directly overhead at one of the stations, the line between it and the station makes a 90° angle with the ground. Then, by use of trigonometric equations, you can find the height of the meteor.

Meteor tracking can also be done by radar methods, although this requires much more equipment and a background in electronics. A radio signal is sent out on a transmitter. When it hits the meteor trail, part of the radio energy is reflected back to a receiver near the transmitter. Actually, the radio or radar waves are reflected by the column of ionized gas left in the wake of the meteor.

Using electronic methods, the elapsed time of the radio pulses' flight can be measured. This gives the distance to the meteor trail. Other methods determine the strength of the echo and lead to the measurement and location of radiants and to the velocity of the meteor.

One advantage of tracking meteors by radio is that such activity can be pursued during the daytime. Four daylight meteor showers have been detected that are at least as spectacular as those listed in the table.

If this field of research is one you would like to delve into seriously, you can contact the American Meteor Society. They have stringent membership requirements but are particularly interested in encouraging radio research in this field. For more information, write to:

Dr. David D. Meisel, Director
Dept. of Physics and Astronomy
State University College
Geneseo, N.Y. 14454

12

TINY PARTICLES

COLLECTING MICROMETEORITES

The tiniest members of the solar system are very small metallic or rocky particles. They are only a few microns in diameter (a micron is 10^{-4} cm). Some of these are from the debris left behind by comets as they orbit the sun, but similar particles are also found in less abundance throughout interplanetary space. Unlike the larger meteoroids, these "micrometeoroids" do not burn up from their interaction with the molecules of air when they enter the earth's atmosphere. They are too light in weight for that. Instead, they are slowed down by the atmosphere and float gently down to the surface. They are then called "micrometeorites."

It is estimated that up to 100 tons of micrometeorites enter the earth's atmosphere every day. We are not aware of them because they enter with a minimum of disturbance. However, they can be distinguished from the normal dustfall that pervades our atmosphere.

More micrometeorites are found in the atmosphere after a meteor shower (see the list of meteor showers in Chapter Eleven) because the earth has swept through a much heavier concentration of these particles than it normally encounters in its orbit around the sun. The particles' light weight sometimes keeps them suspended in the air until they are washed out by rain or snow. They can then be collected and examined. But first they must be separated from the rainwater and from the dust particles that are of earthly origin.

Because these tiny particles fall to the ground during a rainstorm, the easiest way to collect them is to first collect rainwater in a dish. Use a flat, shallow pan such as a 12-inch (30-cm) pie plate. There may be dust or dirt particles already in the pan, so line it first with clean aluminum foil or plastic wrap.

Plan to collect rainwater before and after a major meteor shower. In that way you will be able to measure the increase in cosmic fallout during the meteor shower. If possible, collect rain before and after the richest showers, such as the Perseids (August 9–14) or Leonids (November 14–18).

To collect metallic micrometeorites, sweep the bottom of the rain-filled pan with a magnet. Because they are rich in iron, the particles will adhere to the magnet. If you first place the magnet into a plastic bag, it will be easier to remove the particles later without harming them. Place the covered magnet with all the particles clinging to it into another clean, shallow dish or pan that you have filled with distilled water. This should also be lined with aluminum foil or plastic wrap to avoid contamination by other particles.

While the covered magnet is in the distilled water, remove it from the bag and gently swirl the empty plastic bag around, allowing all the particles to fall off. They will settle to the bottom of the dish.

Sweep the rainwater several times in this manner to collect as many particles as possible. The distilled water must now be evaporated and the particles dried out. The quickest way to accomplish this is by boiling off the water. If you plan to do this on a stove top, you should, of course, use aluminum foil and a metal pan, but if you use a microwave oven, be sure to use a Pyrex dish and plastic wrap. If the pan must sit for any length of time, cover it with a fine gauze to prevent any dust from falling into it.

Once the particles are dry, collect them with a magnetized needle. (A needle can be magnetized by rubbing it on a magnet several times in one direction.) Put the particles on a microscope slide and examine them. A 100-power microscope is necessary for smaller particles, but a magnifying glass may be enough for some of the larger ones.

Once you have several collections of metallic particles, you can start sorting them according to size and shape. By taking samples before and after the meteor shower, you can make comparisons of the size, shape, and number of micrometeorites collected on each date. The particles collected before the shower are your "control" group. Although some of these may be from space, it is likely that many are from industrial pollution here on earth.

Particles in both the before and after samples that appear similar are most likely from the earth. Look for those in the after-shower sample that have a different appearance or size. These are probably from space. In general, the number of earthly particles stays relatively constant, whereas the number of cosmic particles varies throughout the year. By collecting particles during each rain over a period of several months or more, you will obtain a large sample and be able to make better classifications and identifications.

Once the metallic particles have been removed from the rainwater, the remaining particles can be collected. But first the water in the pan must be evaporated, just as the distilled water was. Boil the water off and allow the leftover particles to dry, covering the pan with fine gauze to prevent dust contamination.

The particles that remain in the lined pan after the

rainwater has been evaporated are nonmetallic. You can use a wet, nonmagnitized needle to pick them up. Put them on microscope slides to be examined.

Although some of these nonmetallic particles are, of course, from the earth, many are not. They are stony micrometeorites, a far more numerous variety than the metallic ones. Like the much-larger stony meteorites, stony micrometeorites are much harder to identify than their metallic counterparts. But by using the same method of collecting and classifying before and after meteor shower samples, you may be able to distinguish the terrestrial particles from the micrometeorites.

Be sure to keep very accurate records, with dates of all rain collections. Label all your slides. If you can photograph the enlarged micrometeorites by attaching a camera to your microscope, such an exhibit will add greatly to your project.

DETECTION OF COSMIC RAYS

Throughout space there are very high-energy particles that are believed to have come from erupting stars such as supernovae. Most of these particles are electrons, protons (hydrogen nuclei), and alpha particles (helium nuclei), although a small percentage are the nuclei of heavier elements. They are all moving at velocities approaching the speed of light.

These particles are called "cosmic rays" because they were originally thought to be photons of energy rather than minute bits of matter. Although they may originate from specific stars, they are deflected in their paths by magnetic fields that exist throughout the universe. For this reason, they appear to come from all directions, and their origins are very hard, if not impossible, to detect.

When they hit the earth's magnetic field, those particles with the least energy are deflected along the lines of the magnetic field and interact with the earth's atmosphere only at the magnetic poles. But the more energetic particles break through this magnetic barrier and interact with the atoms and molecules of the upper atmosphere all around the earth. The atoms and molecules in the atmosphere are broken up, causing great numbers of them to be knocked downward by the impact. They, in turn, hit other atoms and molecules with the same effect. The collisions cause great showers of free electrons and nuclei to rain down upon the earth. These secondary particles also have very high energies.

Normally, we cannot see either the primary or secondary particles, but it is possible to detect their presence when they pass through a cloud or bubble chamber or through a radiation counter such as a Geiger counter. You can make a simple cloud chamber and record and detect these particles.

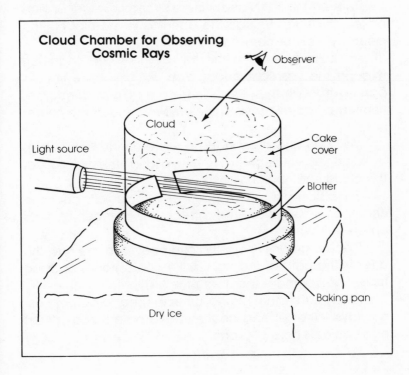

Cloud Chamber for Observing Cosmic Rays

Observer

Cloud

Light source

Cake cover

Blotter

Baking pan

Dry ice

Place a piece of black cloth in a round metal baking pan or pie tin. Instead of using black cloth, you can paint the floor of the pan with a flat black paint.

Take a transparent bowl or cake cover whose rim fits inside the pan, and line its inside wall with a long strip of blotter material. Make the strip just long enough so that there is a 1-inch (2.5-cm) gap. The blotter should not completely line the inside wall of the cover.

Pour methyl alcohol over the black cloth until it is thoroughly soaked. There should be at least ⅛ of an inch (about 3 mm) of alcohol in the pan. Put the bowl or cake cover over the pan so that the blotter is sitting in the alcohol. It will soak up the liquid quickly.

Place the pan over some dry ice so that the alcohol vapor is cooled. A cloud will form inside the bowl as the vapor cools to the point of supersaturation.

Turn off the lights and shine a strong flashlight or slide projector beam through the opening in the blotter. The cloud will now become quite distinct.

Look down through the top of the cloud chamber, through the flashlight beam. You will see white streaks passing through the cloud. These are trails of condensation left by cosmic rays as they move through the chamber.

You can photograph these white condensation trails by setting up your camera to take a long time exposure of the cloud chamber.

Try placing a watch painted with radium near the chamber. How does that affect the number of trails observed? Why?

Place a magnet near the chamber, and see how this affects the path of the trails. Take photographs of these trails, and compare them with the first ones.

Investigate other methods being used to detect cosmic rays. What effects do they have on our bodies? On other objects here on earth?

13

VARIABLE STARS

Although most stars shine with a constant luminosity, a significant fraction are known to vary in brightness. Their periods of variability range from less than a minute to over a year. And their changes in brightness can be anywhere from as little as a fraction of a magnitude to ten or more magnitudes. These stars are called "variable stars" or just "variables."

There are thousands of known variables, and many more are still being discovered. Their study is important because, depending upon the type of variable, their changing luminosities can tell astronomers about the star's mass, radius, temperature, composition, internal structure, and evolutionary stage.

Professional astronomers do not have the time or the observing time on a telescope to monitor the changing brightnesses of hundreds of stars night after night, and therefore this is a field in which the amateur astronomer with very modest equipment can make a significant contribution. Many students have used such observations as their science fair project and then have continued to observe their chosen star or stars, adding to their observation program as time and experience permitted.

To set up an observing program of variable stars, you must first be very familiar with the sky and know the constellations well. A star atlas can be of great help here. There are several excellent ones listed in the Appendix. The only observing instrument necessary is a telescope. This can be of any size and, in fact, for observing the brighter variables, a good pair of binoculars is all that is needed. Then, with suitable star charts and a lot of perserverance and determination to succeed, you are ready to begin.

Luckily, there is an excellent organization dedicated to encouraging and aiding variable-star observers. This organization is the primary source of information on all aspects of variable-star observation. It is called the American Association of Variable Star Observers (AAVSO), with headquarters at 187 Concord Avenue, Cambridge, Massachusetts 02138.

AAVSO has a program that includes observation of two thousand variable stars of all types. It has finder charts for almost all of them. These are available at minimal cost to member and nonmember alike. An example of such a chart is shown on the facing page. As you can see, a very small section of the sky is shown on such a chart. You must first be well acquainted with the brighter stars in that particular area of the sky before trying to use these charts. That is why a star atlas is of such great help.

AAVSO publishes its own atlas as well as a list of other suitable ones. It also has other publications that will help you get started and then progress to more advanced levels of observation. If you are interested in observing variables with a photometer rather than visually, AAVSO even has a manual that contains instructions and diagrams for building one and instructions on how to use it.

However, most beginners start with visual observations of variables. Besides articles and pamphlets on how to start your research, AAVSO will also recommend variables for the beginner and for the more experienced. Eventually, you will be able to set up your own observing program, selecting those stars that interest you the most.

061317	(d)	**Sample AAVSO Chart**	

Sample AAVSO Chart

UY CANIS MAJORIS

Scale 20" = 1mm

1900 06^h 13^m 51^s − 17° 02′2
2000 06^h 18^m 18^s − 17° 02′2

Sp GDv   Type RVa   Per 114^d Mag 10.8-12.8^e

061417	(d)	

UZ CANIS MAJORIS

1900 06^h 14^m 21^s − 16° 59′9
2000 06^h 18^m 47^s − 17° 02′0

Sp MGII   Type SR   Per 82^d.5   Mag 11.0-12.3v

Obs. 1968-1970 indicate star "a" = var, 11.0-11.9
"b" = var, 11.1-13.0 (CES)

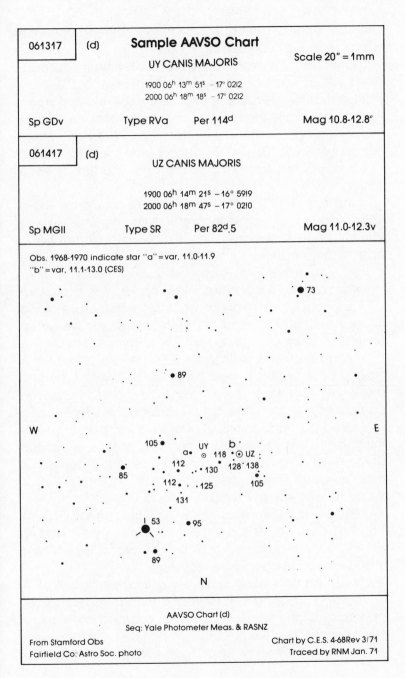

W

E

N

AAVSO Chart (d)
Seq: Yale Photometer Meas. & RASNZ

From Stamford Obs
Fairfield Co: Astro Soc. photo

Chart by C.E.S. 4-68Rev 3/71
Traced by RNM Jan. 71

The frequency of your observations will depend upon the star or stars that you select.

Of course, it is expected that you will submit your data to AAVSO so that they can add it to the rest of the information that they receive from observers all over the world. It then makes all of these reported observations available to professional astronomers for their research. Make copies of all your observations and send them to AAVSO headquarters as soon as possible after the first of each month.

The first variables that you observe should be those whose periods of variability are well known. This will give you the necessary experience. Pick a variable that has a bright star nearby that you can find in a star atlas. If the star is bright enough to be seen with your naked eye, finding the variable will be that much easier. You can point your telescope to the bright star, and with the use of the finder star charts, start moving from one distinctive group of stars to another until you zero in on the variable.

To determine the brightness of the variable at the time of observation, it must be compared with a nearby star whose brightness doesn't vary. It is important that the comparison stars you use are those suggested by AAVSO, so that your estimates can be combined with others. All of this takes time and great care and may seem very difficult at the beginning. But there are many ardent observers all over the world who started in the same way and are now ready to help you continue the work.

For more information about this field, AAVSO published a book in 1980 entitled *Sky and Telescope Guide to the Heavens.* It describes their star atlas and how to use that atlas to observe variables.

You can also study variables photographically. One advantage of using photography is that thousands of stars both bright and faint can be recorded on a single photograph. Then this photograph can be compared with earlier ones of the same field to see which stars varied and by how much. The majority of variables have been discovered in this way. The brightness of the variables can be measured by measuring the size and density of the photographic image.

In richly populated regions of the sky, such as the Milky Way, this is a particularly efficient way to study many variables. The use of the Blink Method, which is described in Chapter Sixteen, can help detect variables very easily in such a field.

Photoelectric techniques are the third method of studying variables. You can make your own photometer or purchase one from a scientific supply house such as Edmund Scientific. Electronic components are not very expensive today, and individuals as well as schools and organizations can have such equipment. If care is taken, very accurate and useful results can be produced.

The photometer will record much smaller brightness changes than can usually be detected by other methods. With the use of color filters inserted into the light beam, small color changes can also be investigated. Because of its ability to detect minute luminosity changes, hundreds of "microvariables" have been discovered with the photoelectric method. These microvariables represent new classes of variable stars that could not have been discovered by visual observation.

14

THE TIMING OF OCCULTATIONS

Every month, as the moon moves through the twelve constellations of the zodiac, it naturally passes in front of a number of stars. Such a phenomenon is called an "occultation." Technically, an eclipse of the sun or moon is also an occultation but, of course, a very special kind.

There are two parts to every occultation of a star by the moon—the disappearance and the reappearance. Each of these events, the disappearance and reappearance, are timed as accurately as possible by trained observers. Their timings are then used to determine a more precise position of the moon. This in turn enables astronomers to learn more about the earth's nonuniform rotational speed.

At each of the two timed moments, the limb of the moon is on a line (tangential) connecting the star and the observer. Then, if the position of the observer and the star are known exactly, the position of the moon's limb at that very moment can be calculated.

Although it is the professional astronomer who ultimately uses the data to determine the earth's rotation, the observations and timings of occultations is another area in which the amateur astronomer can make truly valuable contributions. Your observations and that of the professionals are given equal attention, because no large or expensive equipment is needed. And most professional observatories are too busy with other research to devote much time to this activity.

Every year, lists of predicted occultations are published in the *Astronomical Almanac.* If you cannot obtain a copy of this reference book, you will find occultation information in the *Observer's Handbook,* a yearly booklet put out by the Royal Astronomical Society of Canada. Astronomy magazines also carry occultation predictions each month.

Note that these printed listings are only predictions. There are many perturbations of the moon in its orbit so that actual positions may vary slightly from the predicted ones. That is why the observations and recordings of occultations are so important.

With the help of lists of predicted occultations, you must first select a star that lies in the moon's orbit. The phase of the moon does not matter. However, unless the star is very bright, the full moon may make observations difficult. Most lists of predictions use stars that are brighter than +7.5 magnitude. These can be observed easily with a pair of binoculars or a small telescope. Only during a lunar eclipse can fainter stars be seen.

If the moon is a crescent, when the star disappears or reappears on the dark side of the disk, the event can be quite startling. Within only about 1/10 of a second the star blinks out in what appears to be dark, empty space. The rapidness of the disappearance is because the moon is moving rapidly from west to east among the stars, and the occulted star is only a point of light in the sky.

With more sophisticated equipment, such as a photomultiplier tube and a high-speed recorder, the diminishing intensity of the starlight at successive instants can be measured, but such equipment is normally beyond the reach of the average amateur astronomer.

Every hour the moon moves in the sky a distance

equal to about its own diameter. Therefore, the longest time possible for an occultation is an hour. Of course, the time can be shorter if the star does not pass directly behind the center of the moon. Therefore, it should not be difficult to record both the disappearance and reappearance of the star if weather permits.

In order to accurately time and record an occultation, you must first know your position on the earth to an accuracy of one second of arc, or about 33 yards (30 m). That means that if you move your telescope more than a few meters or yards, you may have to determine another set of coordinates. To pinpoint such a specific location, large-scale maps are usually available at reference libraries or at a surveyor's office. You must also find your altitude above sea level.

The Bureau of Standards, Station WWV, and the Naval Observatory broadcast a continuous standard time signal for the continental United States. Station CHU in Ottawa, Canada, and WWVH in Kauai, Hawaii, also broadcast time signals. If you have no way to listen to the seconds beat from these signals as you observe, you can use a stopwatch, starting the watch at the moment of occultation but then referring to the broadcast time signals as soon as possible. You may have to devise your own method of timing the occultations. But be sure to explain carefully how the timing was accomplished.

Although you will want to keep your data for the science fair or other competitions, copies of it should be sent to the world clearing house for occultation data as soon as possible. Otherwise it will never have any value to the astronomical community. The address for all occultation data is:

H. M. Nautical Almanac Office
Royal Greenwich Observatory
Herstmonceux Castle
Hailsham, Sussex, England

When observations for one full year have been received from observers all over the world, they are fed into a computer to determine the differences between the moon's actual and ephemeris (predicted) positions. Then the difference between Ephemeris Time and Universal Time can be calculated. This difference is caused by the nonuniform rotation of the earth.

The record of any occultation observation should include the following data:

1. Identification of the occulted body.
2. Time of the occultation and/or reappearance. This should be correct to $1/10$ of a second, although errors are likely to be at least plus or minus 0.2 seconds. State if time is U.T. or local.
3. Your exact latitude, longitude, and altitude.
4. Description of your telescope—type, focal length, diameter of aperture, power of eyepiece.
5. Method of observation and timing procedure, including source of timing control.

There are other types of occultations that can be observed. A planet is sometimes occulted by the moon, although this is a much rarer event than the occultation of stars. Because a planet is a disk, its light is not cut off as quickly as a star's light. The data from such occultations is used to check the exact value of the Astronomical Unit.

An even rarer event is the occultation of a star by a planet. These can only be seen through relatively large telescopes, and astronomers must sometimes travel to distant places to view them.

15

"STAR GAUGING" THE MILKY WAY

When the Milky Way that we see in the sky was discovered to be made up of thousands of stars, astronomers started comparing this area with those that were not as populated. In the eighteenth century, William Herschel actually counted the number of stars he could see through his telescope in 683 selected regions. This "star gauging," as he called it, led him to the conclusion that the sun lay inside a huge, disk-shaped star system.

You can repeat Herschel's research either with or without a telescope, although with a telescope you will be able to see many more stars all over the sky and resolve the multitude of stars in the Milky Way region. However, without a telescope, look at different parts of the sky through a tube. This will limit your view of the sky to equal areas. Do this throughout the year to cover the entire plane of the Milky Way and the rest of the sky. Observe only on clear, moonless nights and only after your eyes have become adjusted to the darkness. In each location of the sky carefully count the number of stars you see through the tube. If you can mount the tube on a sturdy tripod so that it does not move while you are counting, the task will be much easier.

In the winter, observe an area east of the constellation Orion. Compare the number of stars in this area with the number in the bowl of the Big Dipper. In summer you

THE CONSTELLATION OF ORION
AND ITS SURROUNDING STARS

can concentrate your attention near Scorpio and again compare the figures with those from the Big Dipper region. These are only suggested regions, of course. Use any that are easy to observe during the selected season of the year. Be sure that you include an area within the Milky Way region.

You will find that the stars are less numerous in the "winter" part of the Milky Way than in the "summer" part. Why is this so? What does it tell us about our position in the Milky Way Galaxy? Can you locate the direction of the center of the galaxy based upon your findings?

The Milky Way that we see in the sky is, of course, the plane of the galaxy. It is the "galactic equator." The points 90° away from the Milky Way are the North and South Galactic Poles. Can you locate the North Galactic Pole? How does this point differ from the North Celestial Pole?

The ratio of the number of stars in an area of the Milky Way to the number of stars 90° away is called the "galactic concentration." This ratio goes up as larger and larger telescopes are used. It is only 3.5 for the brighter stars that can be seen with the naked eye, whereas it is 40 when using the 200-inch (5-m) Palomar telescope. This huge instrument can detect forty times as many stars in the Milky Way as there are in an equal area near the galatic poles.

Some areas of the Milky Way have a greater concentration of stars than other parts. One in particular, the one looking directly toward the galactic nucleus, has the most stars. This is because we are not at the galactic center but way off to one side of the galaxy.

16

BLINKING

Blinking in astronomy is not a motion of the eyelids but rather a simple method of detecting things that change in the sky. These include variables, of course, but can also be the means by which you discover a nova or a comet. Blinking also allows you to see planetary motions.

You don't need to know all the stars and constellations, nor do you need very costly equipment. What you do need is:

1. a 35mm camera with a 50mm lens or, ideally, a 135mm telephoto lens, and some high-speed film;
2. two slide projectors of the same make;
3. a small 120-rpm "synchron" motor, which can usually be obtained from an electrical supply house; and
4. a home-built device that will hold the two projectors.

The idea is to take duplicate photographs of selected sky areas over a period of many months or even years. By centering your viewfinder on a specific target star, the photographs will all be of the same field. Use exposure times of about two minutes so that the star trails won't be too long. If you have a clock drive, you can use longer (five-minute) exposures. This will yield more stars to study. Once you have taken a number of duplicate star fields, you are ready to "blink."

Load two different slides of the same star field into separate slide projectors, and project the images onto a screen so that they overlap as precisely as possible. You will want to build some sort of device that holds the projectors in correct alignment so that you don't have to constantly be checking this..

By rigging up the synchron motor with a rotating shutter in front of it, you can rapidly cover first one projector lens and then the other. A 120-rpm motor will give you sixty views of each slide every minute, constantly alternating them on the screen. However, to the eye, it will look like one projected image—except for the things that have changed.

These objects will immediately draw your attention because they will seem to be blinking on and off or jumping back and forth as one and then the other slide is projected onto the screen. You can test this method and your setup by photographing a star field containing a planet or an asteroid and then taking another photograph of the same star field a few weeks later. The asteroid or planet will seem to jump back and forth if the two images are correctly aligned.

The more photographs you take, the better records you will have to compare your newest shots against. And you may just be the first to find a nova! or a comet! This is also an excellent way of detecting Pluto and is the way this most-distant planet was discovered.

PLUTO MOVING AGAINST
THE BACKGROUND OF STARS.
THE TWO PHOTOGRAPHS
SHOWN WERE TAKEN
TWENTY-FOUR HOURS APART.

A word of caution: There are all sorts of moving objects in the sky, some unknown, but most very well studied. It is a good idea to establish contact with some knowledgeable person at a nearby college, university, observatory, or planetarium with whom you can check your findings. This will avoid any embarrassing false alarms. It is also a good idea to take two photographs of the same star field every time to rule out any tiny film defect that can look deceptively like a star, a comet, or even a nova.

For more information about blinking, you can write to Ben Mayer, 1940 Cotner Ave., Los Angeles, California 90025. Mayer started an organization to coordinate blinking participants in an effort to thoroughly cover the entire sky. The organization is called PROBLICOM, which stands for *Pro*jection *Bli*nk *Com*parison.

17

ADDITIONAL
IDEAS

There are many other experiments and projects in astronomy that you can consider for your science fair project. To describe each one in great detail would require a far bigger book than this one. However, here are some additional suggestions. Several of them you will be able to do without very much assistance or outside equipment, whereas others will require the use of laboratory or observatory equipment. Perhaps one of them will suggest another avenue of research that will interest you even more.

ASTROPHOTOGRAPHY

The camera is one of the main tools of the astronomer. Photographic plates can reveal objects too faint to be seen by the naked eye because long time exposures enable the camera to collect and record far more light than the eye is capable of doing. Also, the photograph becomes a lasting record that can be used by researchers many years from now.

The use of photography has been mentioned in several projects, but here are some other ideas:

- Using color film, photograph various types of stars.
- Make a star atlas.

STONEHENGE, ON THE
SALISBURY PLAIN IN ENGLAND

- Compare the photographs of a star field taken first with a red filter and then with a blue one.
- Illustrate the apparent daily motion of the stars by photographing star "trails."
- Photograph throughout the year as many of the Messier objects as you can locate.
- Using photographs of star trails, compare their lengths according to their declinations, and from this data calculate the earth's sidereal period.

ARCHEOASTRONOMY

Ever since Stonehenge in England was found to be an ancient astronomical observatory, scientific interest in prehistoric monuments throughout the world has increased. One of the most famous in the United States is the Bighorn Medicine Wheel in Wyoming. A study of the astronomical alignments of this type of ancient ruin and its implications as to the scientific knowledge possessed by the early peoples who built them would make a fascinating research project. A model of the ruin would be a necessary part of any such project.

POTPOURRI

When Galileo first pointed his very primitive, homemade telescope toward the heavens, he made more discoveries about our universe than had been made in the two dozen centuries before him. Describe and illustrate one of the following astronomical discoveries and discuss its importance to science:

The four major moons of Jupiter
The phases of Venus
The craters and "seas" on the moon
The rings of Saturn
The multitude of stars in the Milky Way

Demonstrate how astronomers use trigonometric parallax to determine the distances to the nearby stars. Calculate the distance to some faraway terrestrial object using this method. What methods are used for calculating distances to the more distant stars? How do these methods relate to the trigonometric parallax method?

Determine the resolution and limiting magnitude of a telescope. Compare the size of its field and the various magnifications of several lenses. For what astronomical observations is each the best? Why is a high degree of resolution important in astronomy? Why must radio telescopes be so much larger than optical ones? Does the size of the telescope or the amount of magnification determine the degree of resolution? Why?

Study the stellar distribution in open-star clusters, in globular-star clusters, or in the region of the Milky Way or the celestial pole. Count the numbers of stars of each spectral type and note star sizes in each area studied.

Make observations and take measurements of binary stars using astrophotography and a micrometer.

Make observations and take measurements of eclipsing binary stars by using a photometer to determine the stars' orbital elements.

With the use of prisms, show how white light can be dispersed into a rainbow or spectrum and then recombined into white light again.

THE PLEIADES, AN OPEN-
STAR CLUSTER. NOTE
THE NEBULOSITY STILL
SURROUNDING EACH STAR.

THE GREAT NEBULA IN THE
CONSTELLATION OF ORION

Write a computer program to:

> determine planetary orbits
> measure absolute magnitudes of stars
> compute planetary or stellar masses
> determine galactic distribution of the stars
> solve the three-body orbital problems
> determine the path of a space probe to a given
> planet

Study some phase of stellar evolution, such as the composition of protostars in nebulae. What are stars made of? What is their main energy source at various stages? What is the energy source, for example, in planetary nebulae? These projects may require professional equipment and should not be undertaken unless you have access to proper facilities.

18

CONTESTS AND COMPETITIONS

There are many contests and competitions that you may enter with your science fair project. Of course, the science fair being held at your school is the first such contest to consider. The most outstanding projects from each school's fair are usually brought together at a regional fair, where they are judged against each other. Then the best of these are selected to enter the State Science and Engineering Fair. In each of these events, the Outstanding, First, and sometimes Second Place projects are advanced to the next level of competition.

For high school students, the culminating event is the International Science and Engineering Fair (ISEF). This "world series" of science fairs is held annually in May, with student contestants from affiliated fairs in the United States and elsewhere. Two students from each affiliated fair are chosen to represent their district.

More than 450 awards are presented at the ISEF. General Motors Corporation sponsors the ISEF Grand Awards, which are given to winners in twelve different disciplinary categories. GM also awards two students with an all-expenses-paid trip to the Nobel Prize ceremonies in Stockholm, Sweden. Many other organizations and corporations give special awards for work in a variety of disciplines. These categories are determined by the organization giving the award.

Being chosen as a contestant in the ISEF also enhances a student's chances of admission to the better colleges and universities. College admissions officers look favorably upon such extracurricular activities, which show originality, persistence, and initiative. These traits are important for success in a scientific career.

More information about the ISEF can be obtained by writing to the International Scientific and Engineering Fair, Science Service, 1719 N Street. N.W., Washington, D.C. 20036.

Some other programs for high school students are sponsored by:

Junior Science and Humanities Symposium, Academy of Applied Science, 4904 Waters Edge Drive, Suite 268, Raleigh, N.C. 27606.

Mr. Roy Cowin, Executive Director, JETS (Junior Engineering Technical Society), 345 E. 47th St., New York, N.Y. 10017.

London International Youth Science Fortnight, 9 Grosvenor Gardens, London SW1, England.

Junior Academies of Science, American Association for the Advancement of Science, 1515 Mass. Avenue, N.W., Washington, D.C. 20036.

THE PRISCILLA AND BART BOK AWARDS

These annual awards are specifically for high school projects in astronomy. They are chosen on the basis of originality, skill, inventiveness, and significance of results. A five- to fifteen-page description of the project, in the style of a serious scientific report, is required. This should include references, figures, and diagrams. Examples of suitable projects include the design and construction of instruments or pieces of equipment, astronomical measurements, or a theoretical computation of some aspect in astronomy. For more information, write to Professor Michael D. Papagiannis, Chairman, Department of Astronomy, Boston University, Boston, Mass. 02215.

THE WESTINGHOUSE
SCIENCE TALENT SEARCH

The Westinghouse Science Talent Search is perhaps the most famous competition open to high school students. It is sponsored by two institutions, the Westinghouse Electric Corporation and Science Service. Its objectives are to find and to help educate those students whose scientific or engineering research skills, knowledge, talents, and abilities indicate creative potential. The awards also make us aware of the role that science and engineering play in our lives.

Although there is no age limit, you must be in your last (senior) year of secondary school. To enter, you must submit a report of about a thousand words on an independent scientific or engineering research project. Other information about you and your school record are also required. There is a very firm deadline for your entry (usually December 15).

The forty top contestants are awarded invitations to the Science Talent Institute. Ten of these are then selected to receive four-year Westinghouse Science Scholarships. Westinghouse Science Awards of $500 each are awarded to the remaining thirty contestants. Three hundred other entrants are given Honorable Mentions, and recommendations are sent to the colleges, universities, or technical schools of their choice. The awards and scholarships are given on the basis of the quality of the independent research report, scholastic and personal records, and any other information assembled by the judging committee.

Many states have their own State Science Talent Search, which is held concurrently with the national competition. This enables hundreds more students to receive recommendations and other assistance toward a college education and a scientific or engineering career.

To enter this competition, your science teacher or some other school official must request the entry materials from Science Service, 1719 N Street, N.W., Washington, D.C. 20036. For further details, ask your science teacher for a copy of "Science Talent," or write to Science Service at the above address.

If you are interested in competing in one of these contests, do not let anyone discourage you. Even if you don't win a coveted award, the very experience of participating in a competition is extremely valuable. And you don't have to be a scientific genius to win. Some of the projects suggested in this book are ones that high school students have actually presented at science fairs. A few have won awards. So can you. Good luck!

THE SPACE SHUTTLE AND YOU

Now that the space shuttle is in full operation, NASA is looking for experiments and projects that can be taken aloft on their shuttle flights. NASA officials have set up a program for secondary schools called the Space Shuttle Student Involvement Project (SSIP). This is an annual competition open to high school students only and is run by the National Science Teachers Association (NSTA). Thousands of entries are submitted every year, and the number is steadily growing.

Selections are made according to how clearly written, well-organized, and creative each proposal is, and how well it fits into the space shuttle program. Experiments in such fields as biology, astronomy, behavioral and social sciences, earth sciences, physics, and engineering are welcome. For more information, ask your science teacher or write to NSTA at Space Shuttle Student Involvement Project, National Science Teachers Assn., 1742 Connecticut Ave., N.W., Washington, D.C. 20009. And if you are looking for some ideas and guidance as to how to start such a project, see the companion book in this series entitled *THE SPACE SHUTTLE,* written by Gregory Vogt.

APPENDIX

SCIENTIFIC SUPPLY HOUSES

American Science Center, Inc., 5700 Northwest Highway, Chicago, Illinois 60646. 312/763-0313. (They also have a catalog of surplus items such as optics and scientific materials and small motors. Write for "Jerryco" catalog.)

Edmund Scientific Co., 101 E. Gloucester Pike, Barrington, New Jersey 08007. 800/257-6173.

MAGAZINES

Astronomy, Astro-Media Corp., 625 E. St. Paul Ave., Milwaukee, Wisc. 53202

Mercury, Astronomical Society of the Pacific, 1290 24th Ave., San Francisco, Calif. 94122

Sky and Telescope, 49 Bay State Road, Cambridge, Mass. 02238

Telescope Making, Astro-Media Corp., 625 E. St. Paul Ave., Milwaukee, Wisc. 53202

ORGANIZATIONS

American Association of Variable Star Observers (AAVSO), 187 Concord Ave., Cambridge, Mass. 02138

Bok Awards: Professor Michael D. Papagiannis, Chairman, Department of Astronomy, Boston University, Boston, Mass. 02215

International Scientific and Engineering Fair, Science Service, 1719 N Street, N.W., Washington, D.C. 20036

Occultation Reports: H.M. Nautical Almanac Office, Royal Greenwich Observatory, Herstmonceux Castle, Hailsham, Sussex, England

PROBLICOM (Projection Blink Comparison): Ben Mayer, 1940 Cotner Ave., Los Angeles, Calif. 90025

Space Shuttle Student Involvement Project, National Science Teachers Association, 1742 Connecticut Ave., N.W., Washington, D.C. 20009

Westinghouse Science Talent Search: Science Service, 1719 N Street, N.W., Washington, D.C. 20036

REFERENCE SOURCES, STAR ATLASES, AND CATALOGS

AAVSO Star Atlas. Twenty black and white charts, 12 × 15 inches (30 × 38 cm), unbound, stars to 6th magnitude, Epoch 1900. $6.

Astronomical Almanac (was *American Ephemeris and Nautical Almanac* until 1981). Published annually in U.S. and Britain. In U.S., issued by Nautical Almanac Office, U.S. Naval Observatory. Contains data for astronomy, space sciences, geodesy, surveying, navigation, and more.

Burnham's Celestial Handbook by Robert Burnham, Jr. Data grouped according to constellations includes information about thousands of celestial objects; 3 volumes, $8.95 to $9.95 each, paper. Available from Dover Publications, Inc. 180 Varick St., New York, N.Y. 10014.

Observer's Handbook. Published by the Royal Astronomical Society of Canada, 124 Merton St., Toronto, Ontario

M4S-2Z2. Published annually (1983 price: $6). Data on occultations, brightest and nearest stars, variables, sunrise and set, moon rise and set, etc.

Sky Atlas 2000.0. Available in color or black and white, stars to 8th magnitude; also shows Milky Way, clusters, nebulae, and galaxies. Deluxe (color) edition: $34.95. Available from Sky Publishing Corp., 49 Bay State Rd., Cambridge, Mass. 02238.

Sky Catalogue 2000.0. Lists stars to magnitude 8.0 with right ascension, declination, proper motion, radial velocity, magnitudes, spectral type, distance, etc. Paperbound $29.95, available from Sky Publishing Corp. (see address above).

INDEX

Adler Planetarium, 29
American Association of
    Variable Star Observers
    (AAVSO), 90, 92
American Meteor Society, 82
Analemma, 15
Andromeda Galaxy, 30
Apollo II, 66
Apparent solar time, 13
Archeoastronomy, 107
Asteroids, 57
Astrolabe, 8
Astronomical Almanac, 95
Astronomy, radio, 21
Astronomy projects, 4
Astrophotography, 105, 107
Azimuth, measuring, 5–9

Bighorn Medicine Wheel, 107
Blinking, 101–104
Blink Method, 57, 93
Brightness of stars. *See* Vari-
    able stars

Canals, Martian, 62
Catalogs, reference, 118–119
Centaurus, 23
Cicumference of earth, 67–72
Comet, Halley's, 73, 75
Comets and meteors, 73–82

Computers, use of, 34, 36
Contests and competitions,
    112–116
Cosmic rays, 86–88
Cratering, 48, 51
Craters, volcanic, 51

Daytime star, 37
Diffraction gratings, 24

Eclipses, 94; lunar, 44, 46–47;
    solar, 41
Ephemeris position of moon,
    97
Equation of time, 13
Equator, galactic, 100
Equilibrium of stars, 34
Eratosthenes, 67

Flares, 42
Flashlight pointer, 31
Fraunhofer spectrum, 41
Fusoris, Jean, 8

Galactic concentration, 100
Galactic equator, 100
Galactic poles, 100
Galileo, 17, 53
Geiger counter, 87
Gnomon, sundial's, 10

Great Nebula, 110
Greenwich, England, 13

H II regions, 32
Hale telescope, 18
Halley's Comet, 73, 75
Hayden Planetarium, 75
"Head" of a comet, 77
Herschel, William, 98

International Science and En-
    gineering Fair (ISEF), 112

Jovian moons, 57, 63
Jupiter, 53, 56, 57; moons, 63–
    66
Jupiter effect, 57

Latitude, determining, 10
Leonids meteor showers, 84
Local Group of galaxies, 34,
    35
Local Supercluster, 34
Lunar eclipse, 44, 46–47
Lunar orbit, 46
Lunar surface, 47–48
Lunar terrain, 49

M-type stars, 32
Magazines, reference, 117
Mariner mission, 50, 54, 59–60,
    62
Mars, 53, 61; canals, 62;
    "riverbeds," 59, 60
Mean solar time, 13
Mercury, 50, 52
Meteorites, 48
Meteor showers, 79–82, 84;
    chart, 80
Meteors and comets, 73–82
Meteor tracking, 81–82
Micrometeorites, 83–86
Milky Way, 32–33
Model construction, 32–36

Moon illusion, 47
Moons, Jovian, 57, 63; Jupiter,
    63–65; observation of, 44–
    51
Moonscape, 3-D, 47–48

National Aeronautics and
    Space Administration
    (NASA), 75, 115
National Science Teachers
    Association (NSTA), 115–
    116
Naval Observatory, 96
Neptune, 57
North Star, 10

O-type stars, 32
Objective mirror, telescope's,
    19
Occultations, timing of, 94–97
Optical telescope, 16–20
Organizations, reference,
    117–118
Orion, 98, 99, 110

Palomar telescope, 100
Particles in solar system, 83
Perseids meteor showers, 84
Photoelectric technique, 93
Photographs, use of, 92–93,
    105, 107
Photometer, 93
Photomultiplier tube, 95
Pioneer 10, 56
Planetarium, 28–31
Planetology, 1
Planets, observation of, 52–66
Pleiades, 109
Pluto, 57, 103
Polaris. See North Star
Priscilla and Bart Bok Awards,
    113–114
Projection box, 37–38
Prominences (sun), 42

Ptolemy, 53
Pyrheliometer, 42

Radar, use in tracking meteors, 81–82
Radiant, 79
Radiation, sun's, 42–43
Radio astronomy, 21
Radio observations, 32–33
Radio telescope, 21–23
Radiometer, 42
Reference sources, 118–119
Reflecting telescope, 16, 19. *See also* Optical telescope
Right ascension of stars, 33
Riverbeds, Martian, 59–60; model, 60
Roemer, Olaus, 65
Rotator, 71

Salisbury Plain, 106
Saturn, 57, 58
Scientific supply houses, 117
Schiaparelli, Giovanni, 62
Scientific reports and projects, necessary data for, 3
Sextant, 5
Size of earth, measuring, 67–72
Solar constant, 42–43
Solar eclipses, 41
Solar quadrant, 68
Solar surface, observing, 37–38, 40
Solar system, model of, 59
Solar time, mean, 13
Sources, reference, 118–119
Space Shuttle, 115–116
Space Shuttle Student Involvement Project (SSIP), 115–116
Spectrogram, 24
Spectrohelioscope, 42

Spectroscope, 24–27, 41–42
Star atlas, 90, 118–119
Star chart, 3-D, 33–34
"Star gauging," 98–100
Stars, classification of, 24; variable, 89–93
Station WWV, 96
Stellar spectrum, 24, 25
Stellar structure, 34–36
Stonehenge, 106, 107
Sun, 37–43; photographing, 41; spectroscopic observation, 41; radiation of, 42–43
Sundials, 10–15
Sunspots, 38, 39, 40
Supernovae, particles from, 86
Supply houses, 117

Telescope, Hale, 18; optical, 16–20; Palomar, 100; radio, 21–23; reflecting, 16, 19; transit radio, 22
Telescope-making, 16–23
Theodolite, building of, 5–9
Transit radio telescope, 22

Universal time (U.T.), 38
Uranus, 57

Variable stars, 89–93
Venus, 53, 54
Viking mission, 59–60
Volcanic craters, 51

Westinghouse Science Talent Search, 114–115

X-ray sky, 31

Zeiss Planetarium projector, 29
Zodiac, 94